TOTEM OF THE DEPRAVED

NICK ZEDD

2.13.61

P.O. BOX 1910 · LOS ANGELES ·
CALIFORNIA · 90078 · USA

•

ISBN 1-880985-35-7

2.13.61 Publications, Inc.
P.O. Box 1910
Los Angeles, CA 90078

Printed in the United States of America

For information regarding the films of Nick Zedd write to:

NICK ZEDD
c/o PENETRATION FILMS
PO Box 1589
New York, NY 10009

"The policeman's riot club functions like a magic wand,ZXXZ under whose hard caress the banal soul grows vivid and the nameless recover their authenticity——a bestower, this wand of the lost charisma of the modern self: I bleed, therefore I am."

—Carl Oglesby

CHAPTER ONE

I once had a dream that my mother was cut in half. She was crying and bleeding. I was six years old. I grew up in Hyattsville, Maryland, a quiet town near Washington DC. There was a field and a forest of trees behind our house leading to a creek hidden in the woods where I'd go. It seemed to lead to another world. My parents, ordinary people who lived normal lives, had an abnormal son, for which I will always be grateful. I could never be like them. When I was growing up, my father was employed by the government to censor mail, to determine whether printed or photographed material gathered as evidence could be defined as pornographic and if so, whether a successful case could be initiated against the creators and disseminators of this material. My father was a conservative person who lived a quiet existence as a lawyer and a bureaucrat for the US Postal Service.

My mother is a strong-willed, generous and outgoing religious person. My parents provided me with the usual Christian indoctrination that many people are subjected to in this country. At least they didn't beat me or abuse me. Instead, they left me alone to explore my dreams. We didn't get along too well when I was a teenager, but for some reason they couldn't bring themselves to disown me even though I got busted for drugs, burglarized houses, and once stole a bubble gum machine. My younger brother Jon turned out to be quite normal.

When I was in sixth grade, we moved to a different town. The kids there hated me. My new nickname was "Nigger Lips". There was a Jewish girl I had to sit next to in class whom the other students would throw pennies at when the teacher would leave the room, making her cry. These kids had a hatred of anything different. I wondered where it came from. Smaller ones were picked out as targets by the bullies who seemed to be admired by everyone except the kids they picked on. I once stopped a small gang from beating up a kid named "Doughboy", but most of the time, like everyone else, I stayed silent out of fear. I even joined in once when a boy was chased from the bus and had his shirt ripped to shreds by a howling mob of kids.

I got arrested when I was sixteen, hanging out with a tall kid with blond hair named Walter. One weekend a bunch of us were smoking pot in a parking lot when a cop car pulled up. As the cops approached; we tried to walk back to the car. I asked Walter, "What should I do with the dope?" He said, "Just hold onto it." I threw the pot away, but the cops saw me. They picked it up, handcuffed us and took us to the station. They strip-searched me and put me in a cell for four hours. When my parents came to get me, my mother was in tears. The next day, they took me to a barber who cut off my hair.

A couple years later, Walter got arrested for burning a house down and went to prison. I once took LSD with Walter when I was in the eleventh grade. It kicked in during the middle of a basketball game and made the players accelerate and slow down. Walter disappeared and I ended up going home feeling paranoid. In my bedroom, alone in the house, there was nothing I could relate to so I turned all the lights out and tried to sleep. My mother came in the room and told me they'd invited one of my father's war buddies, a two-star general, to dinner. She wanted me to eat with them. I said I couldn't. She asked why.

"I'm sick."

"What's the matter?" she asked.

"I did acid. I've lost my mind."

She then said, "You may never regain your sanity."

She insisted that I go out and say hello to the General. It wasn't easy. I said hello and went back to the room and tripped another twelve hours and finally came to in a cold sweat. I spent the next six months in a state of depression and made a lot of calls to the guy on the suicide hotline. I tried to believe in Christianity and attempted to read the Bible, but fortunately it didn't work. I became a born-again atheist.

I started painting a lot of surreal canvases of deformed naked people flying in the air. I'd show these paintings at art fairs but nobody would buy them. I started making movies where I'd animate toy soldiers being killed by giant flies. I was getting in trouble in school, skipping classes and roaming the streets with a skinny Jewish kid named Tonk Wanger. We'd drive around in a car on weekends looking for girls. During the day we'd skip classes and sell drugs to junior high school kids. One Saturday night, I terminated an evening of driving around and finding nothing by taking Tonk home. He was incensed. "I bet you only fucked two girls in your life!" he said. Tonk was a virgin like me, but he couldn't admit it. No girls would come near us. We had too many zits.

In high school, I got sent to "detention" a lot. I couldn't seem to obey the rules so I'd be sent to a room where I'd have to sit for an hour after school. Finally, I got out of high school and went to Philadelphia College of Art for two years. I hated most of the people there. I became interested in making films again, so I moved to Brooklyn in 1976 and took film classes at an art school financed in part by student loans I never paid back. It was there that I met Donna, a girl who lived in a room next door to mine in a building on Willoughby Avenue.

There was a lot of tension between blacks and whites in the neighborhood, a run-down section of Bed Stuy. Living there, if you were white, meant being subjected to a lot of bigotry from blacks. I was harassed on a daily basis. I got attacked by a gang once and had to have my eye stitched up. Girls I knew had been raped. One time I had a stomach ache in the middle of the night and had to walk a mile to the nearest hospital, doubled over in pain. The doctors told me that I was getting an ulcer. When I came back, I told my roommate Todd and he told Donna. I thought Donna was a fool. Mentally, she seemed to be living in the Summer of Love. When she heard I was sick though she came over. She parted the curtains surrounding my bed and talked to me, inviting me to come visit her next door when I felt better. She kissed my bare chest and left. That night I went next door and we made love.

I began to visit Donna every few days. She couldn't make up her mind if she wanted to be with me or her Japanese boyfriend, Duane. I discovered that Donna went through a lot of pain when she was a child. She had an older sister who was her best friend and died of cancer when she was five. She had another sister who died of cancer before she was born. She still cried about her older sister. She hated her father who used to beat her, but she stayed friends with her mother. Donna was a painter and she had a lot of talent. After spending more time with her, I felt an incredible feeling of release. All the years I had spent alone feeling ugly and worthless seemed to be over. I gained a new confidence from being with her and she became my best friend. She soon broke up with Duane and I moved in with her.

I gave her the lead role in my first feature, *They Eat Scum*. She played a juvenile delinquent named Susie Putrid who, with her band the Mental Deficients, started a movement known as Death Rock, consisting of kids running around cannibalizing people and causing a core meltdown at a power plant, irradiating the city of New York. The film was horrible. When I shot it, the camera was often running at the wrong speed, turning the actors into cartoon characters.

I showed *They Eat Scum* at Max's Kansas City and Club 57 in the fall of '79. 1979 was a time of renewed energy in the New York film scene. Simultaneously, people who didn't even know each other were making low budget super-8 features starring members of local bands. I would go to the New Cinema, a storefront on St. Mark's Place equipped with a video projector. They would show super-8 movies by Eric Mitchell, James Nares, Vivian Dick and John Lurie. Max's would show the films of Scott and Beth B. in between bands. Meanwhile, I was showing *They Eat Scum* at places like Tier 3 and O.P. Screen, a room on Broadway that had shown Amos Poe's and John Waters' early films. The owner, Rafik, was an early supporter of underground movies and the only curator left from the sixties who was still open minded enough to show the movies of the "para-punk cinema".

I met David McDermott, the diminutive star of *Rome 78*. He was a skinny painter who dressed in clothes from the turn of the

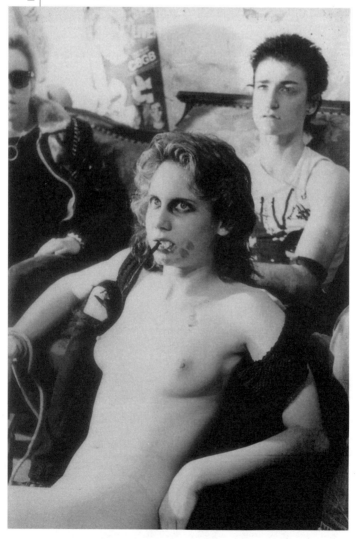

century and drove around town in a souped up Model-T. He became the star of my 1980 film *The Bogus Man* before submerging into his fantasy of living in the year 1900. Lydia Lunch was appearing in films while playing around in a succession of noise bands. Her band Teenage Jesus and the Jerks would do ten-minute sets while the audience screamed, "Less!" Before the club scene was corrupted by overpriced tickets and the invasion of out of towners, CBGB's and Max's were a vortex of energy with bands like the Cramps, the Ramones, Suicide, Richard Hell and the Voidoids, Blondie, Steel Tips, the Blessed, the Contortions, James White and the Blacks, DNA and others who played almost every night of the week. Club 57 was the best club in town, with joke bands, drag queens, old TV cartoons, Japanese animation, fake rappers, lady wrestling tournaments, underground cartoonists and filmmakers and a succession of pre-sellout weirdos like John Sex, Wendy Wild, Klaus Nomi, Ann Magnuson, and an endless list of exotic hipsters and shitfaced lowlife in the days before gentrification ruined the neighborhood. Club 57 lasted until 1983 when, under the tutelage of a junkie with itchy fingers, it succumbed to mismanagement.

My films started getting covered in the *East Village Eye*, *Soho Weekly News*, *Damage* and other punk publications. I was even denounced on the front page of the *Wall Street Journal*. A tape of *They Eat Scum* was shown in Germany to an incredulous and silent audience. I wanted Lydia Lunch to be in my next film so I met her at Tier 3 and she said she'd do it. We agreed to meet at a certain time so I got a cameraman, but when we arrived at her apartment, she wasn't there. She'd left town. I didn't see her again for three years.

After making *The Bogus Man* in 1980, I was living on welfare and moved into a loft on West 35th Street with Donna and a guy

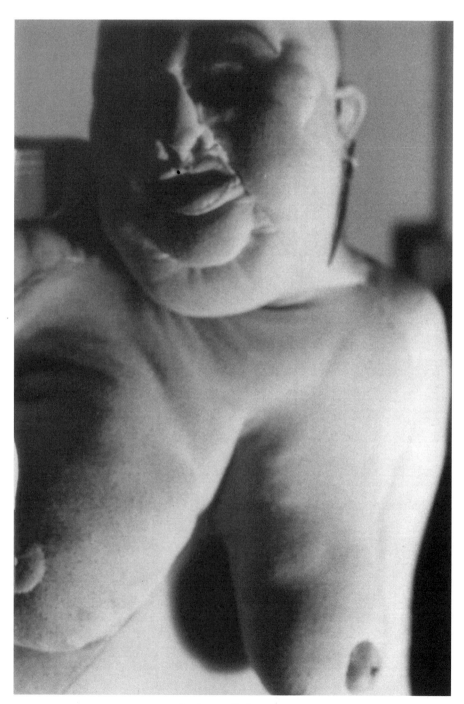

GRIER LANKTON IN "THE BOGUS MAN"

named Screaming Mad George, a ridiculous painter who fronted a band called The Mad. We shared the place with his entourage of Japanese friends. I was showing *They Eat Scum* weekends at O.P. Screen when I got cut off from welfare. I got a job as a bike messenger, but I kept wrecking the bikes when cars would hit me. I broke my elbow and became a foot messenger. I left resumes at every film company in New York but nobody would hire me. I went to the three major networks and offered my services but they weren't interested. I called ABC and asked, "Do you need any educated people on your staff?" The person who answered replied, "Very funny! Who do you know here?" I said, "Nobody. What does that matter?" She said, "Don't you realize, it's not WHAT you know, it's WHO you know?" "Well you don't know anybody so FUCK YOU!" I screamed.

Desperate, I went through the want-ads and found a job at a Haagen Dazs. When I got there, they asked me how many years experience I had with an ice cream scoop. "How many do you need?" I asked. They wouldn't hire me. Nobody would. They all said I was overqualified. Flat broke, I went home to live with my parents in Maryland. I got a job as a washroom attendant in a porno theater for three months before getting fired. Returning to New York, I got an apartment with Donna on 11th St. and Avenue A, then tried for a year to get grant money to make films. I was, however, about to meet the man who was to be my greatest influence—Jack Smith.

CHAPTER TWO

Unlike most people, I suffer from an obsessive mental disorder that has made me think I can be a motion picture director without being a multimillionaire. In a perverse way, I have accomplished this. But at what cost to my sanity?

The only family I now have are my movies. These movies are enormously unpopular and with each new monstrosity, I create a more hideous distortion of "reality" and a more real expression of what I am. I have tried to release my id in my films—to express something beyond words—my own confusion and horror, joy and ecstasy at being alive. These deformed, brilliant, and beautiful entities are shadows of light and sound made to cut through the hypocrisy to which you and I are conditioned.

Unreasonable expectations were planted in my brain when I was five years old and saw *Voyage to a Prehistoric Planet*. I was stunned and traumatized by the thought of being shipwrecked on a planet of dinosaurs and cavemen. Little did I know this was to be my destiny.

Thanks to my obsession I became a hermit. I tried to visit the vomitorium of mediocrity that passes for our world and I once almost believed that I was in touch with real people. But a chillingly mindless cheerfulness was incomprehensible to me, especially when imposed by a series of bad jokes. The squealing noises people make to children and cats are also incomprehensible to me—they appear to be faked—and the smug cynicism and insulting innuendoes of the carrion I know make me want to puke.

Several years ago, angered by the spiteful film critics at the Voice and other publications who blacklisted me for the crime of criticizing their indifference, I devised a plan to subvert their ignorance by launching a movement known as the Cinema of Transgression. Publishing a magazine called The *Underground Film Bulletin*, I wrote a series of manifestos lauding the emergence of new films by people like Nazi Dick, Tommy Traitor, Manuel Delanda, Erotic Psyche, and a plethora of others, most of whom betrayed the movement years later in acts of petty jealousy and heroin induced fraud. The plan worked for awhile and journalists and curators temporarily woke up and paid attention to films they'd been ignoring for years. Sooner or later though, almost every filmmaker I'd mentioned in articles or included in group shows ended up stabbing me in the back, lying to me, or accusing

me of exploiting them by exposing their work to more people. Some, in their jealous treachery, went so far as to write falsified biographies of me which were then printed in nationally circulated magazines as my "obituary". I was astonished at the vehemence of their jealousy and the absurd lengths to which these pedalogical pipsqueaks would go to discredit me. Nobody seemed to notice how much their limited

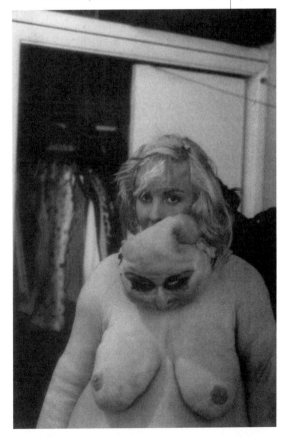

fame depended on my clandestine support so I decided to drop the traitors and let them flounder on their own.

In the nightmarish debacle of bringing the Cinema of Transgression to life, the only things that didn't betray me were the films I made. I have since devoted my energy to the creation and dissemination of these films to my eternal regret.

The awareness that the outside world is resolutely committed to going backwards bothers me. I see it every time my roommate turns on the TV. The person I live with spends hours in front of it watching programs which are crude propaganda for a "normal" point of view. All conflicts are cheerfully resolved with a fake sincerity by boringly ordinary people oozing a pustulent sentimentality. That every cliché on TV is met with a hail of applause and laughter reinforces the illusion of democratic consensus. But how could someone like me turn the poison of mass sedation around?

I discovered that being an underground filmmaker makes me less than nothing. With the world corroded by an entertainment industry that is so restrictive and reactionary and so motivated by

ZEDD & SUSAN MANSON / R. KERN

an urge to please a contingent of cretins, I feel no more influential than a homeless person asleep in front of the White House. Why I had to find an activity designed to obliterate the values of the dominant hierarchy is beyond me. Why couldn't I be happy just driving a cab?

Being an independent filmmaker is a baroque curse. It means none of your films will likely be reviewed by anyone and only a tiny fraction of the general public will ever know you exist. I have tried to get my films seen and distributed, but no one will touch them. My "lifestyle" has become an obscene parody dictated by endless games designed to con people out of money so I can puke out a few more turkeys before I die. The only people I have anything to do with are my investor and my roommate, two strange creatures I've been trying to get away from with no luck.

It has taken me ten years to find somebody to be my investor. This person is a commercial artist who would rather be doing something avant-garde but is unwilling to sacrifice material comfort in order to accomplish this goal. This person lives vicariously, enabling me to create my masterworks which make no money and are hated by everyone.

Recently, I thought if I made a movie where everyone was naked I might get laid. The film, entitled *War is Menstrual Envy*, would deal directly with the misdirection of my sexual energy. Two of the actresses on the project might have wanted to fuck me but for some reason didn't feel right about it. I thought if I played an octopus, I might be able to rape Annie Sprinkle but Kembra Squalor insisted on doing the scene instead and would only allow her husband to rape her. I thought up another scene where I'd play a mummy and have sex with an old girlfriend, but she had band practice the night we were supposed to do it so I had to give the scene to two other actors. I pray I will find some way to get laid before this film is done since it is costing my investor so much money.

My roommate spends more time talking to cats than to people. Every penny I raise driving a cab goes to pay Baby Jane Holzer, ex-Warhol superstar turned greedy slumlord. My rent is three times what it should be. These sixties superstars are now parasites leeching off poor creatures like me, stealing our architecture and selling it back to us at fantastic prices.

A couple of years ago, in a vain attempt to protest the murder of Michael Stewart by a gang of transit cops—who were later exonerated by our evil judicial system—I made a film called *Police State*. It demonstrated the lengths to which the state will go to exterminate those who deviate from the approved cultural stereo-type. Since making the film, I have tried without luck to get it seen in America and Canada where it was twice stopped from being shown by government censors. In New York, no theater will exhibit

NICK ZEDD AND KEMBRA PFAHLER IN "WAR IS MENSTRUAL ENVY" / KATRINA DEL MAR

the film and I have been repeatedly turned down for any grants to finance future work. When I took *Police State, War is Menstrual Envy* and another film called *Whoregasm* to show in Washington DC, only three paying customers showed up. I spent six hours the night before putting up posters all over the University of Maryland and downtown DC. No newspaper would mention the films and a heavy snowstorm occurred the night of the show to keep people away.

Maybe someday people will care about underground films, but I doubt it. That's part of the definition of being underground now. Nobody cares. In the face of a mad rush to be normal, most Americans won't bother to go see anything out of the ordinary. I have accepted this. In our present era of mindless complacency and profound ignorance, America, the great Fascist Empire, is controlled by multinational corporations dedicated to the destruction of diversity, and in their stampede to crush the deviant, urban planners and corporate gentrifiers have made enormous gains at the expense of those aspirations of the human spirit to which all civilizations are ultimately judged. One day, the transient concerns of our national corporate oligarchy will vanish into dust along with the military industrial complex which sucks up such a disproportionate amount of our people's money. In a thousand years, like any civilization, ours will be judged by the ideas found in the subterranean artifacts being produced by the impoverished and the marginalized, and it is for this reason that I continue to make films whether or not anyone comes to see them, because they speak to me and to future generations who will one day dispose of this monolith of greed that oppresses us all.

CHAPTER THREE

In 1981, I met the underground filmmaker Jack Smith who directed *Normal Love* and *Flaming Creatures*, "a masterpiece of inane kitsch" back in the sixties. He lived in a tiny sixth floor walk-up jammed with garbage and decorated to look like a kindergarten version of Baghdad. The bathroom was a lagoon filled with plastic vines. His bathtub was filled with moss. He planned to film a pirate movie with miniature ships in it. The door frames were modified with spackle to resemble Arabian arches and the place was crawling with roaches. He kept his movies in a closet in the kitchen under his bunkbed.

I used to come over to help him paint the walls of his "set". He would take time out so he could make tea. He sat at the kitchen table and placed the package of tea in front of our cups. As soon as he opened the package at least twenty roaches came scurrying out. He remained oblivious to their presence and asked me how much tea I wanted as he stuck the spoon in the box. I said, "None," as I watched him drink it.

One night I was at his place with a Cuban filmmaker named Ela and we decided to go out. He wanted to put on "exotic attire" before leaving and came out with a pair of hideous, striped platform shoes which I convinced him to wear and an Arabian scarf which he affixed to his head. In the platform shoes he stood at least seven feet tall. He made an attempt to descend the six flights of stairs but tripped and fell before he could make it to the fifth floor. He took off the shoes and left them in his apartment. Smith had a paranoid obsession, fixating on a man he called "Uncle Fishhook", a filmmaker named Jonas Mekas who he claimed had stolen his films and was sucking him dry. "Uncle Fishhook stole my roachcrust," he'd mumble. He had a rolodex in which were scribbled cryptic messages like, *It's no use...I'm too old...I have no more pasty cheerfulness...* and *Unexotic Aftermath of Nuclear Hollow Crust.* He felt the image of lobsters being boiled alive was a perfect metaphor for man's existence.

Anyone he despised was a "crust"—what was left over after being eaten out—including Andy Warhol, whom he'd made a film with in the early sixties. Everywhere we'd go, he'd get strange reactions even though he was totally passive. When I had to move out of an apartment, Jack came over to help, holding a Chinese umbrella when it wasn't raining. The super, a loud, fat Russian, slammed the door in his face and started screaming hysterically for no reason. When I couldn't reason with the beast, a guy I knew

named Tom went in the vestibule. The Russian suddenly stopped when Tom screamed at the top of his lungs, sounding more insane than him. I was impressed since Tom was only five feet tall and the Russian was six foot two. He finally let us enter the building, but it was Jack's passive weirdness that set him off.

I wanted Jack to play a college professor in one of my films and he insisted that he'd memorized the script

JACK SMITH (1989) / CLAYTON PATTERSONH

but it was essential that I purchase a pair of glasses for him from a junk store. I asked how he would be able to see with the wrong prescription. He said if we looked hard enough we'd find it. We went to all the local thrift stores looking for spectacles—a waste of time since he could just as easily have worn frames with no lenses in them—but he refused, saying they had to be authentic. He planned on making a Sinbad movie in his apartment. When I asked how he could shoot an entire feature in a one room apartment, he said he'd play all the parts to save space. He later decided his stuffed penguin could do a better job.

He wanted to change his name to Sinbad Glick, the Pink Pirate, but then decided it might offend "anti-Semitic pressure groups" so he changed it to Sinbad Rodriguez. He said one day he planned to burn all his films so nobody would steal them. He had an expensive 16 mm camera he'd been given by some camera company which grew dust in his closet for years. When it came time to rehearse a scene, he showed up at my place without his glasses and said he couldn't see anything so we went to his apartment.

Jack Smith (1989) / Clayton Patterson

When he put the glasses on, he revealed that he hadn't memorized any of the script and tried to cover it up by attacking its literary merit. He was incapable of rehearsing the scene with the other actors since he refused to take it seriously, reciting the words on the page in a monotone voice so we left Jack sitting in his room staring at the sheets of paper. "Don't you want them back?" he asked as I left.

I never saw Jack smile the entire time I knew him, but he was constantly trying to get other people to laugh. He told me once, "In Europe, I danced with a penguin. I was paid an enormous amount of exotic currency and was treated as royalty. The penguin was inert and feeble and at the conclusion of our dance I inserted my finger in his rectum. I smelled my finger. It did stink." He would tell me stories like this in a sad whining voice and a completely straight face. He thought he was "unphotogenic" and wanted to have his nose removed since it was shaped like a hook. I'd tell him it was his best feature but he wouldn't believe it. *I was the world's most glamorous pie crust,* he once wrote. He had a strange charisma and often tried to manipulate people to do all his work for him. He told me at one time he was turned into an "art machine" by unscrupulous "college scum" who fed him drugs so they could exploit his ideas. He once punched out a federal narcotics agent at a poetry reading for attempting to bust someone smoking pot.

Smith was living on bonds purchased with money he'd inherited from his family years ago and complained about the sordid nature of his sex life. He would go to Variety Photoplays and get blow jobs in the balcony seats. He did the same thing at the bath houses and complained of the lack of romance in these encounters. I wondered if I might become a sexual attachment in his eyes and tried not to spend much time with him even though I found the nature of his genius fascinating. I asked him if he had ever been in love with anyone and he said once, but he drove them away. "It was a terrible mistake," he said.

One day, a couple of weeks after I'd spent an afternoon painting gold trim over the arches of Baghdad in his apartment, I called to invite him to a performance I was doing with Nazi Dick and Tommy Traitor at a dive called Darinka. He angrily asked, "Why would I want to go to that?" and made it clear that he considered me a traitor for not visiting him or calling him more often. I told him that he was a flaming turkey. We never spoke after that.

. Every person he knew at one time or another had been subjected to his paranoid wrath and an army of enemies existed in his mind, isolated for decades in his fantasy world on First Avenue drinking bottles of Guinness Stout. In 1989, at the age of 57, he died of AIDS. Someone told me he said it was "a glorious way to die."

Jack Smith was a "failure", but he refused to commit suicide. By refusing to make concessions to everyone else's feelings, he remained pure and uncorrupt, maintaining his individuality in a way that no one else could. He showed me that most people who are "successful" are really shams because they've committed mental suicide through the process of compromise. He proved to me that you can rise above living for other people and that the integrity of one's vision can be maintained even in the face of poverty and indifference if you believe in yourself.

CHAPTER FOUR

The first time I saw Lydia Lunch, I was sitting behind a table in the top room of Max's. The lights went off, the curtains parted and standing in front of me was the most beautiful creature I'd ever seen. A barrage of screeching noise attacked my ears and my eyes were shocked to see a nineteen year old girl in a leather miniskirt with black hair falling into her face, standing five feet away screaming at the top of her lungs with alternating expressions of rage and boredom as she assaulted her guitar. I couldn't believe what I was witnessing. She was like something out of a dream. Her face bore an expression of such profound contempt, I was immediately concerned with how I might be able to make her smile.

I knew then I was in love with her.

When I heard she had moved to LA, I wrote her a letter. She didn't write back and I tried to forget her but I'd be haunted by her image in a magazine as the look of rage on her face seemed to articulate my own feelings of resentment at a world of overbearing mediocrity and mindless drudgery.

Four years later Lydia walked up to me in a night club and said she wanted to talk, gave me her phone number and walked away. As I returned to my apartment that night, I knew a major change was about to take place in my life. I immediately felt an internal confusion as I realized the pain Donna was about to go through. A mixture of despair and elation, guilt and self confidence racked my brain.

The next day I called Lydia and invited her over. Donna had gone to work. My heart was pounding as I walked to the door to let Lydia in. She entered, wearing a leather jacket under a denim vest and a black skirt. She was nervous and impatient and I was surprised to find myself more composed. We didn't say much but went into the bedroom and I sat down on the edge of the bed as she paced the floor. She then stopped, looked at me, leaned over and kissed my lips. As if hypnotized, we fell onto the bed kissing and holding each other. Suddenly, I felt an immediate sensation of nausea. I told her to leave. I told her I'd call soon and when she left, I went to bed in a cold sweat, tormented by an awareness of her power over me.

That night I called and went to her apartment on the fifteenth floor of a building uptown. She took me to her room and stood by the window in a long black dress. I whispered to her, "I love your body." I lunged at her, pressing my mouth to her lips and pulling her hair back and shoved her halfway out the window. She clung to the window frame with one hand as the rest of her body hung out the window. Her life was in my hands as I kissed and sucked her neck. She wouldn't let me push her out without pulling me with her so I grabbed her waist. We landed on the floor and I smothered her with kisses and felt hard as I pulled her face close to mine, grabbing her hair. I caressed her breasts before I ripped her stockings off and pulled down my pants. I rolled her over and plunged my cock into her as she gasped in shock. I shoved it in and out of her cunt as she squealed in pain and I grabbed her hair in back and pushed her face onto the floor.

I rubbed her face in the dirt and stuck my dick as far as I could into her body. A raging voluptuous id consumed us both as I rubbed her face into the floor; the face that ignited my lust, her dark eyes now closed, her teeth clenched tight as I pushed her down further into a smothering pit of shame, an abyss of degradation transcended by the pleasure of our orgasms. As I shot into her, she writhed and squirmed helplessly on the floor. "You're dangerous," she said. As I finally withdrew from her, I felt a satisfaction I had never before felt. I felt immortal, unchained, in love with the most beautiful woman on Earth.

I expected Lydia to be a bitch. Instead, she was interested in testing the limits of erotic conduct. Her intellect far surpassed any woman I had met and she cared more about writing, performing and fucking than in taking drugs and doing nothing. We exposed ourselves to fear as a form of excitement and death seemed to be an element of possibility. Sex with her was an explosion beyond words and we each seemed to mirror the other's mind. I'd never known anyone who reminded me more of myself. We seemed to be psychic twins in some frightening way and I was completely in awe. We wanted to shock the world.

We wanted to do whatever was dangerous and forbidden— something that would place us in the annals of crime forever. When Lydia went to LA for a week, I told Donna that I had been seeing her. Donna couldn't take it. I moved in with Lydia.

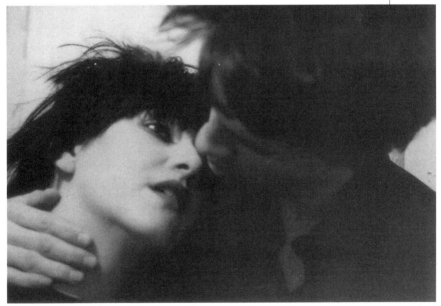

Lydia seemed to have a romantic fantasy of being killed by a lover. She had said in an interview that she was looking for the right person and I thought I was the one destined to do it if that's what she wanted. For some reason I felt poised on the brink of an act that would change my life—that if I didn't destroy her, I was going to end up doing it to someone else.

I'd start crying when I'd see children on the street—their innocence awaiting the rot of society's touch.

Lydia went to London and our plan was for me to go there a month later to live with her. With her gone, I wondered if we were going to actually follow through on our vague idea to victimize someone. I thought if I could kill somebody and get away with it, only then could I know if I was beyond guilt and morality, the two states of mind I was most interested in eliminating. What had I not done? What was I afraid to do? And why should I be afraid to do it? Is it because I think it's right or wrong? I didn't believe in "right" and "wrong". After thinking about it for a month, I came to the realization that I didn't actually want to hurt anyone. I didn't want to destroy Lydia although I felt if she wanted to, she could have used me to commit her own suicide. She seemed depressed enough. Her view of reality seemed to become mine and I didn't want anyone else to have her. Killing her would have been the only way to keep her.

To fulfill our desire to touch death, we talked about kidnapping children in some other country, killing them and filming it, then showing it in America. To do this would be the ultimate perversion of our talents, an act of "absolute evil" that no critic or acquaintance could accept, combining crime and art—two seemingly irreconcilable opposites in a perverse unity. If I could do that and not feel guilt, I would have achieved the ultimate freedom. After thinking more about it, I decided it would be a cheap way to get famous and that I had no right to do it since I didn't believe in taking someone else's life unless they deserved it. I soon realized the ultimate freedom lies in being able to kill someone in your mind. To do otherwise would be an act of cowardice, something I wasn't prepared to live with. I acted out the consequences of killing an innocent victim in my mind and it made me feel remorse before having done it. After going through this mental process, I no longer felt the need to do it.

Lydia invited me to come live with her in London. A month later, I raised the money and took the flight over, but by then, Lydia was no longer interested in me. Our impassioned three month affair which led me to leave my apartment and girlfriend no longer mattered to her. She arranged for me to stay in a girlfriend's apartment since she was now living with one English guy and seeing another. I was very depressed, as I sat alone in London crying and thinking about Donna and how I'd left her. What was I doing here? Lydia kept sending me to different friends' apartments to stay. I was finally sent to a flat owned by a pair of death rockers in Brixton who worshipped Aleister Crowley. They kicked me out after a week when I wouldn't go to a gay bar with them. With nowhere to go, I went to Hyde Park and noticed a girl who was walking with a bike. I liked the way she looked so I started talking to her. She was French and said her name was Natassia. I walked with her to a squat she was staying in with some English people.

When I got in Natassia's room, I immediately made love to her on the floor. Then I moved in with her. In the next few weeks we made love everywhere we could—on the rooftops of abandoned buildings, on the grass, in the woods and on the mattress on the floor in her room. We went to the south of France and stayed at her parents' cottage and then stayed in Paris for a week in her father's apartment. Natassia was awkwardly beautiful and androgynous; exquisite in an unaffected way but she wasn't complex or intelligent and she couldn't fascinate me as Lydia had. She didn't have any interest in seeing the rest of the world. She just seemed to like things the way they were. I couldn't love her so she told me to leave. When I got back to London, I fell apart. I felt so alone, I wanted to die.

I returned to New York hoping that Donna would take me back, but it was too late. She had found someone else. I stayed in

different people's apartments sleeping on their floors until they told me to leave. When I ran out of friends, I slept on rooftops and park benches until it got too cold. A Cuban girl named Iliana let me move in with her. She had a big dog named Zantibee who'd grab people's legs and try to rape them. Iliana was homesteading an abandoned building and I'd go over and pound nails in floor boards with her. She'd give me money if I worked a few hours and I'd use it to buy food. Sometimes I'd show one of my movies in a club and make a hundred if I was lucky.

I edited a movie I'd shot of Lydia in London, got it booked in a big club and made a thousand dollars on it. Then a Cuban girl named Ela asked me if I'd make a film with her in which I would seduce people on camera, re-enacting my method of surviving on the streets. We went out looking for girls to be in the film. In front of Stromboli's on First Avenue, a fat girl asked me, "Are you from England?" I said no and started talking to her. She had a beautiful face and bright red hair.

Gia lived on Bleecker Street her whole life—sixteen years. Her parents, who had long since broken up, treated her like shit when they weren't ignoring her. She'd been living with her grandmother who had just died. I asked her if she'd want to be in a movie and she said yes. The next day I was set to do two scenes: one with Gia and one with Phoebe Legere, a skinny performance artist who for years had been claiming she'd "be on Johnny Carson next week" after her "Playboy spread came out". Without the luxury of a script, I did the scene with Gia in which I examined her jewelry and then handcuffed her and proceeded to undress her until she whispered to me that she was a virgin. I asked her if I could move in with her and she said yes, so I told Ela to turn off the camera and left. Phoebe was pissed since she'd planned to let me move in with her but hadn't told me yet.

The next day, improvising a scene with Phoebe during the filming of the movie, I began to understand Ela's directorial approach. She'd turn on the camera and sit back and let us do all the work. She never gave any direction and we never knew what was going on; I had to figure it all out as the camera was rolling. In a daze, Ela dropped the camera and broke a lens. She must have forgotten she was filming. When she got the film back from the lab, instead of editing it, she just threw it on a projector and pronounced it finished.

Gia and I got along alright except that whenever I'd try to stick my dick in her she'd start screaming hysterically. Sex was out, but I didn't care since she was letting me stay at her place for free. The whole concept of paying for the space you live in, particularly when the guy who built it died hundreds of years ago, flies in the face of common sense so anytime I could get out of paying rent I'd go for it. I seemed to get along fine with Gia even though she was a complete imbecile, but after two weeks I was bored so I moved into the Jane West Hotel and got a job driving a cab. My room was a flea-bitten jail cell made out of cardboard. Welfare winos wandered through the halls. One old man appeared to be wearing a Civil War uniform. People were always arguing through the paper thin walls. "I ain't no alcoholic, I'm a drunk," I heard one guy say. The maintenance man, a fat black guy, would sit naked in the shower on a wooden chair at four in the morning and let the water run on him with a look of disgust on his face. There were no shower curtains.

Driving a cab was paralyzingly dull except on rare occasions. Once I picked up a guy from a hotel on Times Square with a black eye and a bloody nose. A doorman stuck him in the back seat and the guy asked to be taken to Brooklyn through the tunnel. By the time I got to the tunnel, he was passed out. "Wake up! You gotta pay the toll!" I yelled. He wouldn't wake up so I made a U-turn, drove back and dumped him in front of Beekman Hospital. I'd pick up hookers and they'd shout at each other in the back seat, telling me to "take her monkey ass over to Park Avenue," and when we'd get there they'd want to be taken over to the West 50's where there was more business. They loved to drive in circles all night screaming like banshees, but they never gave tips. Totally exhausted after twelve hours, I'd return the cab at 6:00 AM and then take another cab home. I'll never forget looking out the back window of a cab and seeing a Spanish hooker in the morning sun with a phony smile on her face looking straight in my eyes saying, "WANT A DATE?" It was as plastic and evil a sight as I'd ever seen, that perfectly summed up the absurd misery of my life. She was the only person to look me in the eyes in two weeks. Some nights it would be so dead, I'd drive around looking for hookers. One black hooker wore horn-rimmed glasses and alluringly raised her leather mini in the morning rain to reveal a twelve inch prick. "Best in town, sucker," he gleamed between broken teeth.

A black hooker with huge tits would stand in the middle of 44th Street stark naked all night. Driving around, I discovered that rich people are cheap. Why did poor people give bigger tips? I couldn't figure it.

CHAPTER FIVE

Every time I turn on the TV or leave my apartment I'm reminded of what a slithering mass of pulsating excrement the human race is. Especially when I'm forced to be in the same room with one of its less than perfect representatives for an entire weekend.

I speak of none other than the king of farts, Mr. Nazi Dick. To be subjected to his odious presence for more than a few minutes can ruin an entire month of my sordid life. Minutes turn into hours of hellish boredom when Nazi Dick opens his snout to embellish his empty life with more abject hatred for those to whom he owes everything. On the way to the airport, he always makes sure to walk an extra five feet ahead of you so he can appear to be leading the way even though he doesn't have the slightest idea where he's going. Once we get to our destination, say some bastion of misery like Chicago, he always makes sure to jump in the front seat of whatever car we're riding in, in order to give the impression that he's IN CHARGE even though it's up to the poor schmuck behind the wheel to decide where we're going.

I let Nazi perform these sniveling pranks to boost his ego since I know it makes him feel like less of a bozo, and anyone with an inferiority complex as big as his needs all the help he can get. I know he appreciates having me there to remind him of what an asshole he is. I also appreciate the way he brags about how much better a filmmaker, art world ass-kisser and traveling mongoloid he is. Why is it necessary for Nazi Dick to claim the only mattress in our host's apartment, leaving me with an inflatable beach balloon to sleep on in order to prove his imagined supremacy as a filmmaker? Forget that our host, seeing through Nazi's ploy, decided to stay at his girlfriend's apartment, leaving me his king-sized futon in the luxury suite, much to the fart master's chagrin.

The next night, our Chicago hosts set us up in a dingy basement somewhere with no heat, windows, or nite lite for Nazi, who spent the evening trying to think of something good to jerk off to in the dark while I gazed shivering at the eternal blackness of hell for five hours on a rancid, lumpy couch. I could see nothing in the pitch black hole stretching into infinity preventing me from getting up to piss for five hours since I'd never have found my way to the ladder leading to the toilet above without tripping over fifty open paint cans and one dead fart master in this bottomless pit of hate. As we left, Nazi Dick tried his best to run at least five feet ahead of us to give the impression he was leading the way.

Once at the boring airport I made note of the fact that all the female flight personnel looked like poodles with their clipped and layered Farrah do's, fake smiles, and whining cretin voices. Nazi did his best to suck up to the plastic women but needn't have bothered since they were programmed to be nice to us no matter what.

Once back in New York, the rotting stench of Nazi Dick's farts assaulted the air, giving me little trouble in figuring out why his beleaguered "wife" abandoned him three months ago.

Meanwhile, after undergoing a routine gallbladder operation, Andy Warhol was murdered by the negligence of his sleeping nurse, reminding me to stay away from hospitals for the next century if I valued my life. Fortunately for New York Hospital, Chief Medical Examiner Dr. Elliot Gross was on hand to cover the whole thing up like he did Michael Stewart's murder at the hands of T.A. cops some years ago.

Grotesque somnambulistic mongoloids enveloped me in their vomitous theosophy as I gazed spellbound at the TV, watching Rambozo lie to everyone over some scandal while his cronies did their best to outdo each other with untruths and misstatements to their accomplices de press. With Iranscam, Contragate, and religious vomit everywhere, I plunged headfirst into a concentrated dose of TV brainwashing—the most intense in my life—in an attempt to wipe out all memory of the subhuman slimeballs and prefabricated liars masquerading as my friends in the "real" world. I was promised marriage and a child by one such specimen twenty-four hours before being told she never wanted to see me again since she had another boyfriend. Precariously hanging out a window in hopes that I'd save her the trouble of having to commit suicide by giving her a little shove, the "love of my life" proceeded to pelt the visiting band with stale drinks, getting thrown out of the club for smuggling in a bottle of whiskey before concluding her aimless binge by wailing in a pool of tears as she lay in the gutter outside. She then slithered off to a waiting boyfriend she replaced

me with some months earlier. This all made for a night of profound regrets which thirty-five dollars worth of coke and half a dozen kamikazes did little to dispel some two months later in a bottomless pit in Chicago.

But who's complaining? With a color TV, VCR, stereo, six hundred dollar a month apartment, two cats, portable heater and a meaningless job to keep me occupied, who needs friends? Money must be the meaning of life and I hope to hell I get some before I die. Those green pieces of paper will make it all worth it as I scam my way to oblivion, accumulating even bigger piles, more than I ever expected as the suckers keep shelling it out, wallowing in that pool of shit, waiting for the big black curtain to fall, wiping out the putrescent mess for all eternity. Why don't they just drop the load and get it over with? Shit or get off the pot, motherfuckers. Thermonuclear war now. Let's stop kidding ourselves. There's no hope.

CHAPTER SIX

I was shooting a horror film called *Geek Maggot Bingo* in a loft in Williamsburg when I met Rick Strange.

Rick had an incredibly beautiful girlfriend named Gina whom he'd browbeat in public. "You fucking cunt! Who do you think you are? I'm the one in charge! I'm the one who makes sure you don't fuck things up! If you don't pay attention to me I'll ruin your life permanently! You hear me?" he'd say. Someone in the loft told me, "He's dangerous. Don't talk to him." When I was shooting one scene, Rick came into the room dressed immaculately in a black suit. I asked Gina to wear headphones and monitor the sound during a take. Rick kept interrupting to give directions to his brother Gumby whom I'd cast as a vampire. Gumby's method of acting was to look directly into the camera and smile. He was the worst actor I'd ever worked with. I told Rick to stop trying to direct my film and to leave the room. Gumby told me Rick had just robbed a grocery store in Texas.

A year later, I ran into Rick Strange on Ludlow Street. He was with Gina and a spaced out hippie named Nichole who spent her time reading tarot cards and making cheap costume jewelry. Rick browbeat her the same way he did Gina. He now wore a long black cape and a ludicrous goatee. He started boasting of the days when he'd play guitar with Sid Vicious at the Chelsea. He claimed Vicious was a brilliant guitarist—a blatant lie. I told him he should get his facts straight because he was full of shit. Gina later told me how impressed she was that I contradicted Rick because no one else did. Rick was basically a con artist and a thief, but I was fascinated by his ability to tell outrageous lies and then make up convoluted justifications when anyone contradicted him.

He didn't know how to channel his brilliance in any way so he dedicated his life to a campaign of self-destruction involving as many people as he could find.

Gina and I started seeing each other. She told me that Nichole had a two year old son from a previous marriage with a Vietnamese guy who left town without giving her any alimony. Gina, after breaking up with Rick, started going out with a businessman in New Jersey. Somehow Gina got the guy to give them twenty thousand dollars to open up an occult bookstore. Rick spent the money on cocaine, a solid gold riding stick, a crystal ball, a couple of electric guitars and new wardrobe for himself. His proudest possession was a ninja costume which he'd get Nichole to lace him into while he told stories of having won the North American Karate Championship at Madison Square Garden. He claimed to have been awarded six presidential citations for bravery in Korea and stated he had twenty pounds of shrapnel in his one hundred twenty pound frame.

Gina and I visited Rick, Nichole, and her son Leo in their apartment uptown. Gina left early after sharing some acid, mescaline and coke with me in the bathroom. Rick and Nichole kept a small box in the bedroom filled with the twelve thousand dollars they had left to start the occult bookstore. Rick would never touch the box. In order to get the money out he'd browbeat Nichole, telling her she was an unfit mother for Leo, who'd sit and watch. He'd accuse her of betraying his plans to make them rich.

"I'm the only father Leo has ever had. I'm the best goddamn thing that's ever happened to you two and look how you treat me! I'm Leo's sole role model! You're a shitty excuse for a mother. Look

at you! If it was up to you we'd be eating pizza every day! Let me
tell you, I wasn't put on this earth to eat pizza! You've got your head
in the clouds while I'm sweating and slaving to save our lives!"

Rick was permanently unemployed. Nichole would say, "Eric,
we can't spend the money on coke! It's for the bookstore!"

He'd say, "GIVE ME THAT HUNDRED DOLLARS! I NEED THE MONEY
NOW! NO MORE ARGUMENTS! NICK AND I NEED THE MONEY IMMEDI-
ATELY."

She'd finally hand him a hundred dollar bill which he'd go out
and blow on coke.

Rick took me to a gay bar, dressed in an Australian riding
outfit with a feathered cap and riding boots. He now had a full
beard and smoked a corncob pipe.

"I go here all the time," he informed me.

We returned to the apartment and he bullied Nichole into
giving him another hundred dollars so he could go out and buy
more coke. He came back and we snorted lines, then he berated

Nichole for more cash and repeated the procedure two more times. He left, came back, we did the coke and he didn't think it was good enough.

"We got beat. I'm gonna kick the motherfucker's ass," he said and got Nichole to take out his ninja outfit.

She got down on her knees and laced him into the costume while he told me of his exploits as a third degree black belt master in the Korean Armed Forces.

"When I got my Presidential Citation, I met Jimmy Carter," he said. "You know something? Before I shook hands with the motherfucker, I blew my nose in it."

He pulled out a newspaper ad for a Karate tournament and pointed out his name as one of the winners. All the writing was in Korean. He went out in his ninja costume and came back with a dope dealer. Demonstrating a karate move, he had the guy on the floor in two seconds with a boot heel in his face. Rick would spend hours insulting Nichole, telling her what a worthless mother she was and what a fine father he'd been to Leo. Meanwhile, Nichole was supporting the three of them go-go dancing on Times Square. At the end of the day, she'd fork over the cash so Rick could buy himself beer and drink himself into a coma.

Gina was making all of her money as a hooker and kept telling me she'd meet me and not show up. I got fed up and started fucking a drag queen named Bunny who was obsessed with the Brady Bunch.

I then wrote a play based on the life of a junkie I knew named Jessica and portrayed her on stage with Rick and Bunny. Jessica was a beautiful but neurotic girl with a husband and an English boyfriend. She slept in a tent with her lover in her husband's loft.

I was considering putting her lover in the play, but I changed my mind when he didn't show up for rehearsals and replaced him with Rick Strange. The play, *Me Minus You* was based on Jessica's diary, a ludicrous and hilarious document of the squabbles between three junkies. The night I premiered the play, Rick showed up drunk and tore the script to pieces, then made faces at the audience behind my back until I threw him off the stage. He then wandered through the audience looking for his knife and ended up in the dressing room. He called two bouncers "niggers" and was carried out of the club and thrown into the street before the performance ended. As the audience exited from the club, they were met by an angry Rick demanding to be let back in so he could retrieve his bone handled knife.

Rick Strange and Nichole moved into a house in Woodstock. The townspeople didn't like him too much since he was always trying to con money out of whomever he met. Nichole claimed they thought she and Rick were witches. Somehow Rick got a hold of a shotgun which he'd carry into town with him. One night he got drunk and took the shotgun to the house Nichole was living in with Leo, and for some reason started shooting holes in the walls. The neighbors called the cops and Rick was arrested for reckless endangerment. He was put in the Cook County Penitentiary for three months. He later claimed that Nichole had nailed the windows shut, then lit a fire which backed up and filled the house with smoke so he had to ventilate it by shooting holes in the windows. Nichole returned to Manhattan, leaving Leo with her parents in Queens.

Walking down the sidewalk, I ran into Nichole, whom I hadn't seen in a year. She was now pregnant with her second child. She invited me to her apartment and told me about how she'd just married Rick who was still in prison. Once I got into her apartment, she told me she wanted to have sex with me. I didn't want to fuck her while he was in prison but she insisted and in her pregnant state I found her hard to resist so we made love on her sofa. The next day I went with her to the prison to visit Rick. He was scheduled for a court hearing that morning. Sitting in a coffee shop with Nichole before Rick's hearing, I turned and saw a cop walk in. He had acromegaly and his face looked like a monster mask. When he walked in, the waitress behind the counter smiled and said, "Hi, George. How's it going?" Nobody seemed to notice or care he looked like a monster. Nichole had constructed an elaborate mandala with the names of spirits and gods to whom she prayed for Rick's release.

At the hearing, she gave a letter to the judge.

Eric is a good man. He doesn't belong in jail. Please let him out. I'm lonely.

The judge wouldn't release Rick since he was wanted for armed robbery in Texas. Later, the state of Texas refused to pay for his extradition so the earlier charges were dropped. Rick stood in the courtroom hearing the charges against him. He had chains around his ankles and wrists. Later, we saw Rick in the prison visiting room. He'd lost a lot of weight and had some new tattoos. One of the other inmates, a middle aged man, started crying as he spoke to his wife and son. Rick asked Nichole for more money.

Nichole promised me she wouldn't tell Rick we'd had sex, but a month later, when he got out, she did. Fortunately for me, he didn't care.

When Rick got out we went to a club and he spoke of "the androzome"—another dimension he'd visited. He wanted to start

Donna Death and Bruno Zeus in "Geek Maggot Bingo" / Roberta Bayley

his own church and planned to build a "trapezoid room" where he could "brainwash disciples" to give him lots of money. He then shaved his hair into a mohawk, ditched his safari outfit and started wearing the robes of a Franciscan monk. He moved into an abandoned building with no electricity and painted pentagrams on the walls. He said he was president of the Eighth Street Block Association. He had a tattoo on his arm with the name "Lazar", an old girlfriend who now belonged to a skinhead named Harley. When the skins saw the tattoo, they beat Rick up and ran him out of town. Before he left, he broke into an occult bookstore and stole most of the merchandise so he could sell it to the hippies in Woodstock. He showed me a book of Satanic rituals he claimed to have written. The book had no author.

A year later, Rick returned to Manhattan to look for a job. Nichole was living in a roach infested apartment on East Fourth Street with a sixty-four year old woman named Francis. Francis had a boyfriend named Waldo who had just moved out on her. He was living there to have a roof over his head until he could find a girlfriend his own age. Waldo was a twenty-five year old "artist" who absorbed every minute of Francis' thoughts. She decided he was now being possessed by a witch and that she and Nichole would have to exorcise the girl's spirit from Waldo's brain. Nichole and Francis would spend hours studying tarot cards in an attempt to find a strategy to save Waldo. Francis was taking antidepressant drugs and rejected Nichole's pleas to have Rick move in with them. Rick arrived and moved in anyway. After a few weeks, he was so unbearable that Francis told them both to get out.

Francis claimed to have been a girlfriend of Marlon Brando back in the forties. She was working with Nichole doing textile designs, which Rick would proudly show me when they were gone, claiming he made them. Nichole was supporting Rick by go-go dancing pregnant on Times Square. All the money she'd make, he'd spend on beer and pizza. When Francis kicked them both out, I told them they could stay with me in my apartment. I was subletting the place from a girl who lived in France. Rick and Nichole moved into the living room. Nichole told Rick that he had to get a job because she couldn't afford to keep paying for his booze.

Rick said, "I promise I'll get one. But what can I do?"

"Why don't you go to the Pyramid and go-go dance in drag? You could make eighty bucks a night," I suggested.

Nichole hated the idea of cutting Rick's beard off and kept saying, "Eric, I don't want you to be a faggot!"

Rick had Nichole shave the hair off his chest, legs, arms and face. By the time she was done, he was bleeding from head to toe. He put on a dress and fishnet stockings, stuck a ratty wig on his head and got Nichole to cover his face in pancake makeup. Looking like a witch from hell, he went down to the Pyramid in high heeled shoes and danced on the bar where guys bought him drinks all night. In a couple hours, he got so drunk he fell off the bar and failed his audition. He came back loaded and passed out in the living room with his eyes open. He was wearing a torn black slip and his legs were still bleeding. The whites of his eyes were a sickly red as he gazed straight ahead completely unconscious. He appeared to be dead.

The next day he told me he got a blow job in the ladies room for five dollars. Still in drag, he went out again hoping they would hire him at the bar, but instead he spent the night there getting drunk. Walking home, some skinheads saw him and chased him to my building. I was taking a bath when the door burst open and Rick sat next to me crying.

"They're gonna kill me! My God! Do something!" Tears were flowing down his face as he blubbered, "What am I going to do? They're out there now!"

Suddenly I heard a loud pounding. I got out of the tub and went to the door. Through the hole, I could see five skinheads holding sticks.

"OPEN UP! We want the motherfucker in the dress!" one shouted.

"Get out of here or I'll call the cops!" I shouted.

"Open up! We want the motherfucker now!" the voice said as I went to the phone.

Rick ran to the door. "I'll kill the motherfuckers! Let me at 'em!"

He almost unlocked it before Nichole and I ran over and pulled him back. I called the cops.

Rick was a master of bad judgment. He once claimed his Walkman had been stolen by some Puerto Ricans. He went up to some skins on the street and explained, "Those are the dudes that ripped me off. I'll pay you each ten bucks if you fuck them up."

They beat him up instead.

Two days earlier he entered the apartment in tears, weeping over the fact that some cops had just beaten him up. I called Nazi Dick and told him I needed his help getting Rick and Nichole out before the skins broke in.

"We've gotta get Rick and Nichole out of here and send them to his brother's place in Brooklyn. Bring your knife," I said.

He told me he'd be right over. We waited an hour. The cops and

Nazi Dick never showed up so I opened the door and went down with Rick and Nichole. By then, the skinheads had left so it was safe and we hailed a cab. As it pulled up, Nazi Dick showed up smiling, holding his pocket knife.

One day Nazi Dick called up and said, "Let's do a movie."

I said, "What's the plot?"

"I don't know. Just show up."

I went to his apartment, a place where junkies shot up and large sums of money were passed around as drugs were sold. It was a magnet for the weirdest people in the neighborhood along with visiting Eurotrash and other thrillseekers like Slick, a tall black con artist who'd pound on Nazi Dick's door demanding money he said was owed to him. Once in the apartment, he'd bully whoever was there for cash until he got enough for a bag of dope and then split. Nazi Dick bought a gun to keep Slick out and used to load it and click the hammer back behind the door to make him leave.

Once Slick showed up when Nazi Dick was gone and three Italian girls were in the apartment. Brandishing a ten inch knife, he demanded cash from two of the terrified girls. The third one grabbed his wrist, twisted it, got the knife and forced him out of the

room, something Nazi Dick would never have done.

Nazi Dick was better at hiding his addiction than his friend Tommy Traitor who came over and directed a scene in his movie while high in Nazi Dick's kitchen and knocked over an expensive VCR he'd borrowed, breaking it. Tommy was making a movie about an evangelist who brainwashes a bunch of people into committing suicide, and got Nazi Dick to shoot it, giving me a bit part as a psychotic soldier. Everyone in the cast and crew was high on dope and I couldn't stop laughing at the way Tommy would knock over and break objects while attempting to direct. He accidentally lit his only copy of the script on fire, destroying it before the scene ended. He then taped a condom filed with blood to a firecracker and a piece of leather to the back of his head before lighting it so it would look real when I held a gun to his head and blew his brains out. The firecracker blew up before the camera got turned on and splattered blood all over Nazi Dick's wall. It was the only one he bought so we had to redo the shot by faking it single frame with Tommy acting out his death in twenty-four frames. The apartment was covered in blood, vomit, and broken equipment by the time the scene ended.

Nazi Dick started out making movies like Zom*bie Hunger* in which people would shoot up dope and then throw up on camera. Nazi would do shows in nightclubs with a guy named Blood Boy who'd tear his clothes off and pour blood on himself while screaming. Nazi Dick would shoot up onstage and interrogate Blood Boy while forcing him to kiss an American flag. Blood Boy would then recite Amnesty International statistics on torture to give the performance "meaning".

I was performing live *ordeals* in drag, where at the end of the show, Rick and I would pull out cans of hair spray and light matches, turning them into flamethrowers with which we'd terrify members of the audience. In one performance of *She*, I appeared as a woman with a man's voice reciting his obsession with me before coming out with a knife. A smoke machine I rented for atmosphere went out of control and filled the theater with fog which sent the entire audience running into the streets coughing.

None of these plays were ever reviewed by a single paper. Nobody seemed to realize we were just as important as the Dadaists.

At the end of the last performance of *Me Minus You* at the Collective, I pulled out a gun and shot Rick, who had concealed squibs with blood bags on him so the audience would think it was real. After "killing" him, I pointed the gun at the nervous crowd, then turned it on myself, pointed it at my head and pulled the trigger. Nothing happened. The audience laughed. Pissed off, I looked at the gun and put it to my head. When I pulled the trigger the second time, the blank went off, killing me and ending the show. This was in the fall of 1985 when the fire department told the Collective that they could only have fifty people in the place due to safety violations. Hundreds of people were turned away that night. Soon the city closed the place, part of a campaign of harassment against any venue in New York that might really be avant-garde. Combined with gentrification, this had a devastating effect on the artistic community and effectively destroyed what was left of the underground scene.

CHAPTER SEVEN

Around this time I met a film student named Roseanne who had just chopped all her hair off. People thought she was a lesbian. She followed me everywhere and started assisting me in my work. She wanted to change her name and had played a character named Casandra in a film by a skinhead named Dave. I suggested she use this name so she did.

Casandra started taking photos of me and carrying 16mm projectors and other heavy equipment to my shows. I let her sleep on the sofa in my living room one night. She lived in Williamsburg and I didn't want her to have to take a train home at four in the morning. I wasn't remotely interested in her sexually. At the time I was having sex with Nichole and Bunny. One night I was out drinking with Nichole and Casandra was tagging along. I could never get rid of her. She'd just stand there until I'd leave and then she'd follow. Somehow the three of us ended up in my bed. Once before I'd ended up with Casandra and her friend Lung in my bed but nothing happened. I wasn't attracted to either one. Now I was lying in bed with Nichole and Casandra. I said to myself, "If she won't go away this time, I'll have sex with her. But first I'll fuck Nichole." Casandra never showed any real interest in me besides tagging along and it got on my nerves. I thought fucking Nichole in front of her would teach her some kind of lesson.

I then made love to Casandra. It was incredible. I had no idea sex with her would be so satisfying. I didn't feel like fucking Nichole anymore. Casandra and I made love a second time. I practically devoured her, biting, ripping and bruising her all over. She had a unique proclivity for absorbing pain that cemented us together for nine months.

We decided that she would be my slave and I would be her master. We became obsessed with each other. We both wanted to contradict an acceptable, "normal" relationship. Casandra was fascinated by astrology, numerology and witchcraft. She seemed incredibly gullible, but part of her nature was to open herself completely to any new experience, a reckless kind of courage that I liked. Skepticism was not one of her strong points. In an experiment to see how subservient I could make her, I got Casandra to shine my boots on the floor of someone's apartment while I was wearing them. I'd tie her up when we'd fuck. Her body was branded with bruises I made. All this she would encourage. Whatever rules existed, we wanted to violate them.

Casandra had a seizure when she was ten. She thought this meant she had traveled to another dimension. She said creatures waited for her in the other realm where ultimately she would return. When she'd get really drunk, she'd mention Malpie and Dykie, two "entities" she encountered in the other world. She suspected that I might be an angel from the other dimension. She'd exhibit different personalities when she was drunk. She'd go crazy and jump into garbage bins. I'd have to pull her out.

One night, after I got made up in drag, a bunch of us went to a girl named Tessa's apartment, high on dope, vodka and mushrooms. Nazi Dick and Tommy Traitor were there with a few other people and at some point Casandra climbed out of the bathtub and went crazy, attacking me in Tessa's bedroom. She'd repeatedly run at me and I'd keep tripping her and she'd fall. A girl named Amy said I should walk Casandra home so I took her out in the hall. She slid down the stairs of the apartment building head first, laughing. On the street, she kept trying to jump into a huge garbage container and I kept pulling her out. I was wearing a dress and a black fright wig.

When I got to her apartment, she was so drunk she became delirious, tore her clothes off, and started carrying around a big candelabra. She lay in bed nude holding the lit candelabra and dripped hot wax onto her body. I got her to go in the bathtub and started running water on her. She began to recite lines from a Patti Smith song. Even though she was completely out of her head she'd perfectly memorized all the words.

We used to go up on the roof of my building and fuck at night. Sometimes we'd get into arguments in my bedroom and I'd tell her to get out. She wouldn't leave so I'd have to drag her out of the apartment by her ankles and leave her in the hall. Once I did this and went back to bed. Casandra went up on the roof. I lived on the top floor. She kept calling my name. I looked out the window. She was looking down at me from the roof. She said, "I saw myself fall." I thought she might jump off so I went up to the roof. I kissed her and brought her back down to my room as the sun came up. I should have realized this was a test to determine the limits of my power. If I cared enough to prevent her from committing suicide, I couldn't be in complete control. The voluntary subjugation of Casandra's "slavery" was thus an illusion. The symbiosis of the sadomasochistic rituals demanded the presence of both parties. Her importance was equal to mine.

One night I brought Casandra and Gia to my apartment. I tried to get Casandra to give me a blowjob while I went down on Gia. Casandra got jealous and refused. She lay there pouting while I performed cunnilingus on Gia. She then pulled out an exacto knife and tried to stab me in the back. I pulled the knife out of her hand

and cut my name into her arm. Then we tried to go to sleep. Casandra left the room and went into the kitchen and lay on the floor in the fetal position. I couldn't go to sleep. I kept thinking she might come back with a kitchen knife.

Casandra was now hiding in the bathroom. I filled the tub and placed her in it and then sat with her in the warm water. It seemed to calm her down.

Casandra had a friend named Lisa who later changed her name to Lung Leg and became an actress in Nazi Dick's films. For a time, they were inseparable. Casandra got an apartment in Williamsburg with Lung which they shared until the landlord evicted them. One day, Casandra phoned me in tears to tell me the city marshals had confiscated all her possessions and thrown her out of the apartment. She had nowhere to go. I told her she could stay with me, but only if she was a loyal slave and didn't start fights. We argued constantly. She was a mystic. I was an atheist. She was having her horoscope read to her by a warlock whose advice she'd tape and play back to me. She was jealous that I was having sex with other women even though I was discreet about it. She held a grudge against me for having chosen a drag queen over her once and for continuing to see Nichole after I'd had sex with her. I didn't see what the problem was; I hadn't married her. Even though she pretended to be my slave, her ego was so big she thought that I had no right to fuck anyone else.

Once Casandra tried to surprise me by making steaks on a bunch of dirty pots and pans caked with food that had been sitting in the sink crawling with roaches. She didn't bother to clean the pans since we didn't have any dishwashing liquid. "I'm not going to eat this shit. You didn't clean the fucking pans before you cooked it," I said. Enraged, she ran out.

Once we went to her parents' house in Connecticut. They wouldn't let us sleep in the same room. Casandra's two sisters, mother and father were sitting with us at the dinner table. Her father asked me what we'd been doing in New York. I told him about a performance Casandra and I did.

Her father said, "Why would anyone want to do a performance with her?"

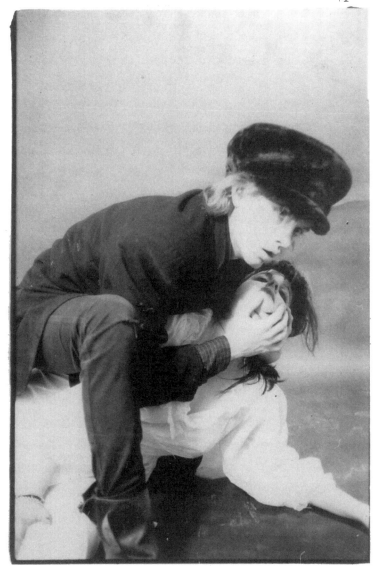

I said, "You don't realize how talented she is. That shows a high degree of insensitivity on your part."

There was a dull silence. Casandra's parents were simple minded people who didn't appreciate her creativity at all.

Her aunt and uncle were having a wedding anniversary that weekend. It was at a Knights of Columbus banquet hall. Casandra and I arrived and were placed at the children's table. Casandra wore a red dress and looked very beautiful. The food and drinks were free so I got drunk. Sitting next to us at the table was a ten year old girl who decided she hated me. When she started insulting me, I insulted her back. Casandra tried to stop me, but I didn't intend to lose a battle of wits with a ten year old. I was amazed when she called me a motherfucker. By the time I called her a whore, a crowd of shocked relatives gathered around us and Casandra dragged me out of the place, drove me directly to the train and told me to get out of town. She said friends of her family were in the mafia and I was lucky to be alive. I didn't understand what the problem was. The kid was a brat. She hadn't shown me any respect, so what was I supposed to do? Somebody should have told her to shut up. After that, we broke up, but we couldn't stand it and were back together within a week. When we'd make love, I'd whisper things that she thought a father would say to a daughter. She accused me of psychologically coercing her by bringing back an authority structure she subconsciously respected.

We'd get along for one day. The next day we'd have an argument and hate each other and be certain it was over. After two days we'd be back together. I'd try to find other girls. I'd go out, get drunk with other people and end up being so desperate at the end of the night, I'd hitch rides to get to the bar Casandra worked at before she'd get off so I could go home with her. I needed her more than she needed me.

It was then that I realized I was a fool.

Casandra would get mad at me for not bringing her along when I'd leave town to do a performance. She didn't seem to understand that I'd want to be alone so I could find another girl to fuck. She became resentful and started seeing other guys without telling me. When she started fucking the warlock, I became jealous. It was embarrassing. I was feeling emotions I was ashamed of—possessiveness, envy and jealousy for anyone who got near her. I knew it was stupid, but I couldn't help it. I felt like she was my creation; that I had molded her into some sort of manic depressive witch that only I could put up with, that only I could console when she went crazy, that only I had the patience to understand. Little did I know the face she was showing to other men. She was a born actress and a slut. Just like me. I never should have accepted the role of her leader since she had to rebel. It was part of her nature. I was just another icon for her to destroy, even though she set me up for it.

I felt helpless over the fact that I couldn't raise enough money to make my own films. The desire to create and the inability to do it filled me with bitterness and resentment and made me look for something I could control, and in Casandra I thought I'd found it, but I was wrong. She now toyed with my love and rejoiced in her ability to degrade me. I'd do anything to be with her, but she no longer cared. She'd tease me whenever we'd meet. I'd buy her drinks all night and watch her dance with other men, then try to walk her home and watch her pick up some stranger at the last minute to remind me of what a fool I was. She led me into thinking we'd reunite while letting a new guy move in with her. I left town to show my films in Ann Arbor never realizing Casandra had found a new lover.

I promised myself I'd be good to her. I'd do anything to please her when I got back. I was changed, but she didn't know it. When I returned, Casandra spent the night with me. We made love and the next day we walked in the snow to an artist's loft in Brooklyn and modeled together in the nude.

I was completely in love with her.

I was sure we could make it work, and for one day, I was completely happy. The next day, she told me it was all over. She had a new boyfriend and he was moving in with her. He was sick and she wanted to be his nurse. I couldn't believe it. I'd never even had a key to her apartment.

I now spent all of my time getting drunk and crying, trying to figure out how not to kill myself. Every time I'd run into her on the sidewalk, she'd flirt with me, then cut me off when she'd had enough. She enjoyed seeing the power she had over me. In my eyes, she became more beautiful. I'd spend hours thinking about her. It drove me crazy. When I'd see her coming, I'd go to the other side of the street. If I looked at her for more than a second, I'd be hooked. She'd follow me and make me stop and I'd be completely in her power. I realized what an imbecile I was, but I couldn't help it. I was addicted to her. Desperate, I tried other women but they couldn't keep me from thinking about her. I thought if I could channel the pain into my work, it would help so I shot my next film, *Police State*, but that didn't stop it for long. I ran out of money and it took me two years to complete it. I was now going through a nervous breakdown.

I decided to write a poem to Casandra...

Dear Cunt,

Thank you for betraying me. It finally enabled me to see how ugly you are.

Beautiful ugly child...why did you leave? May you rot in hell for having run from my love, a hideous specter of insanity caused by your inferiority—which so filled me with lust for you—you fat, useless pig.

I came to worship and pray to your dirty, matted hair and succulent obesity, barely concealed by the torn rags and clownish makeup you wore to please me. I always admired the way you slumped at the bar with a look of total boredom until I walked in. And only I appreciated the bleeding scars bearing my name on your skin after you decided to be my slave.

Dear Beautiful One—You flushed me down the toilet so you could wallow in the shit of an insect's love while my dick was just waiting to explode in your dirty anus.

Didn't you like the way I bit and chewed your flabby flesh like a filthy rabid mutt slavering for a taste of real meat? I put you on a pedestal as my slave and now you deserve to die, but not from my hands. You deserve to be compacted in the anus of a garbage truck sinking in a swamp somewhere disgusting.

Why don't you show these pages to your insect so you can laugh it up and then immolate them at my expense?

You never loved me. Your ego wouldn't allow it. You're probably the biggest liar I've ever met, but you're still the most beautiful thing I've ever known and for this I cry. Because your gentle touch enabled me to feel something. If only you saw how much I loved you. If only you loved me too.

But that can never be, for this world is an insane asylum for idiots like me to cry in and my tears mean nothing to you. You're now as much of a corpse as the rest of this planet, infested with undead beings, performing survival rituals in a somnambulistic regimentation destroying all hope of greatness which only comes from the passion of danger—the kind of danger I hoped to share with you—before you died of cowardice.

So go ahead and laugh. I am now going to find pleasure where none exists. Different from the kind I used to get from destroying all the shit that was in your brain. The pleasure of shedding tears and of being human; of feeling compassion for myself instead of you, who are incapable of returning it. The infinitely superior pleasure of being alone in a world where greatness is shunned for being too repulsive.

You fled from me like a scared rabbit so now you may rot with the rest of the garbage. All I wanted was to hold you and to see you smile; to torment you and to belong to you. To live with you and laugh with you and cry and scream and hate, but most of all, to make love to you in the darkness where we all come from and to which we shall all return.

I went to a party and met a girl named Charlotte who introduced me to heroin, a drug which numbed the pain and for awhile was able to make me stop caring about Casandra. Charlotte became my lover. She was a junkie and she shared her dope with me. Charlotte was the lead singer in an all girl band called Scum Goddess. Her arms were a mass of track marks, deflated veins covered over with trashy leather outfits... knee high boots, red leather jackets and zebra spandex... spikey bleached hair and the face of an angel. Charlotte the Harlot. Charlotte had a .38 caliber Smith & Wesson which I was planning on using to kill Casandra. The gun had no bullets, and I was going to take a train to Connecticut to go buy them, but at the last minute, I changed my mind. I projected myself in a prison cell with a bunch of horny cons sticking their dicks up my ass and postponed my fate. Shooting up dope and coke also helped numb me until I could see straight.

The sight of a thin metal spike as it impaled a thick blue vein made me feel closer to the death that I wanted. The liquid rush of indifference took me away from the jealous rage that sent convulsive shudders through me as I contemplated the loss of the Witch that I loved. The finality of rejection. The finality of memories long past. The total aloneness of being. Always alone. The only time I didn't care was when the dope made me numb. Conscience, guilt and remorse were washed away through a cellular process beyond intellect caused by the medicine I injected.

The intellectual awareness of the futility of unrequited love cannot compete with the chemical imbalance caused by it. Only through a process of self-hypnosis could I forget the body and mind of the woman I loved in order to survive the pain of her indifference. I wanted to die so bad that I cried in sleazy bars. I

cried in crowded streets surrounded by strangers—the ugly, the indifferent, as useless as me or as useful as targets of my hate. It seemed that death was the only escape that was real. I looked everywhere for a myth to believe, an illusion I could love as much as the cunt I no longer had and only blinding indifference could I drown in after the tears. The indifference of dope or alcohol... a suicide by accident... by approximation—or... MURDER.

The sight of Charlotte's face, gleaming a big toothy grin as I squeezed her throat shut with both hands never ceased to amaze me. She enjoyed pain. I could have easily killed her and she would have welcomed it. I just couldn't bring myself. She was a true freak—totally free and real. Thanks to Charlotte's masochism, I found a way to evade my responsibilities as a spurned romantic and avoid killing Casandra even though she deserved it for stabbing me in the back. Charlotte loved having cigarettes put out on her arms and getting bitten by my decaying teeth. I wanted to kill somebody and she was willing to oblige but she didn't deserve it. I probably would have felt different if I were her parents who she sucked dry for dope money, or her mohawked boyfriend Pablo, who I replaced. Charlotte would walk up to guys selling hot dogs on the street and beg them for one and within ten seconds have a free meal. She once went up to a guy selling pussy willows and asked him, "Will you give me some if I show you my pussy?" She'd flash her tits at tourists and poke her ice cream cone in the faces of terrified conformists scurrying down Fifth Avenue. Within a month Charlotte had turned me into a junkie.

After my first withdrawal, I decided I had to stop doing dope. I soon left Charlotte when I noticed the drummer in her band— a girl named Sue Scum whom I let move in with me. I then lost my apartment and was forced to move across town. I took Sue with me. A year later, I finished *Police State*.

I ended up in a dump across town with a shithead for a landlord and a Spanish dwarf for a super. I immediately set to work planning his demise.

CHAPTER EIGHT

He was a walking piece of shit.

He had a pig dog that followed him everywhere he went as protection against the tenants like me who would have stepped on him for being a shitty super. Ask him to turn the heat on in the dead of winter and he'd call you a motherfucker. He stood four feet off the ground. In an ugly squeak he'd shout, "Sooly!" at his wolf pig as he barged into the hall outside my basement dungeon every morning at 5:00. We never got any heat out of the shithead. He put a lock on the boiler and if you called him up, he'd shout obscenities at you for suggesting he do his job. The pipes in the ceiling leaked wet slime that filled the buckets I left on the floors. The cats would drink the rusty slime out of the bowls and get sick. One cat died, but that was probably from eating pieces of the broken dish Sue smashed on the floor during a temper tantrum.

One day a black rat appeared in the toilet. It came up through the pipes and was swimming furiously, trying to climb out, but the bastard couldn't make it. He kept slipping. Sue screamed and tried to flush it down, but the rat was too big and wouldn't go. Her cat looked at the rat and ran away in mortal fear. I got a big piece of metal grating that had fallen from the ceiling when the landlord sent those Spanish mongoloids over to put the ceiling pipes in so we could have the slime fall on our heads.

I held the metal spear over the rat swimming in the toilet and prepared to impale it.

I couldn't wait to hear its squeals and see all the shit filled intestines blotch out in green and red sputum as I chopped through its abdomen, but the cunt felt sorry for the bastard and stopped me. She picked up a scummy dishrag that had been growing mold on the floor and plucked that squealing bastard up and threw it out the window.

Most of the time she'd be sitting in bed stoned, watching TV for fifteen hours after snorting two bags of dope in the bathroom. Life with a junkie is boring. I couldn't justify the money it must cost to lay in a stupor for days at a time. I can do that myself without spending anything.

Sue was far too vain for her own good. She'd always spend ten seconds admiring herself in the mirror behind my head before kissing me goodbye.

I guess I can't blame her. She was an awesome sight. She had a monumental set of tits that helped me get used to the tattoo of a winged griffin covering the skin over her right breast.

I knew she was a bimbo but I loved her anyway because she seemed innocent and honest. Her legs were long and smooth and she had a big ass that I wanted to take a bite out of. She spoke

with a childish speech impediment but so what? She was completely natural, childlike and fragile. She seemed to emanate goodness and I know that sounds corny, but I never felt threatened by her except when she'd knee me in the balls like a clumsy oaf when we were trying to fuck.

At first she'd never let up with the moaning and screaming during sex and that really got on my nerves until I told her to shut up. She got over that soon enough, but then she started with the pain-in-her-cunt routine that I told her to get fixed by seeing a doctor or getting a dildo. He said her problem was mental, but since she couldn't afford a shrink she ended up spending all of the extra cash she made go-go dancing on dope. The dope helped in a way. It made her more horny and took the pain out of her head when my dick entered her cunt.

Our apartment was a prison in hell and the only time I felt free was when a shot of white hot jism came exploding out of my cock. She gave me pretty good blowjobs too, although she'd always get too horny to let me come in her mouth and insist that I jab that fucker into her hole before getting off.

CHAPTER NINE

At noon, a thirty-five year old man stepped out onto Eighth Street between First and Second Avenues buck naked. Couples out for a stroll looked the other way as a thick brown goo oozed out of his anal cavity onto the pavement. The naked man, his cracked skin a charcoal color of built up dirt, was oblivious to the people walking around him as he shit on the sidewalk.

On a park bench on Fourth Street, a black guy with a beard sat motionless. His eyes were closed. Long tendrils of snot, long since solidified, hung from both nostrils, waving in the breeze. The strings of solidified slime were an inch thick and emerged from the two orifices planted in his face. They hung over his blubbery lips, rooting themselves in his greasy thatch of beard. The man appeared to be dead, but I didn't want to get close enough to find out.

A block away, an old bum thrust a paper cup into the faces of people walking down First Avenue, mumbling something about spare change while his cock hung out of the hole in his pants. While walking across Thirteenth Street with Sue, I saw a guy with a mustache pissing next to a cop car. When Sue looked at him, the guy said, "C'mere baby," and smiled. He then put his dick in his pants, opened the front door of the cop car and got in. I noticed his badge as they drove away.

The junkie lies on my bed doing nothing.

She is worthless.

Our apartment is filled with garbage.

I write the word "bad" on her ass.

She does nothing.

She will not do the dishes.

She will not throw out the garbage.

She will not do the laundry.

She will ignore the roaches.

She will die.

Who am I to judge?

I am worthless too.

Because I am with her.

And I will do nothing too.

I am so full of hate it makes me want to explode.

I have tried to accept the monumental triviality of this life. I have tried to reconcile myself to the lunatics, liars and mediocritons who have surrounded me in this world of shit, but it doesn't work. The only thing that can keep me from killing myself is to kill you. I know I'm no better than you or the next creep. It's just that deep down, I can't bring myself to believe it. I'm sorry, but you maggots really are beneath me and I hate you beyond words. I've tried to be indifferent but I just can't. It must be a chemical imbalance. I can't help hating the WHOLE HUMAN RACE.

I had to go somewhere quick after my pig roommate with the fake French accent married an art fag with a beat-up guitar and told me to get out. I stuck her with a two hundred dollar phone bill and skipped town for a month. When I returned, Sue and I moved into a basement on 17th Street with the dwarf super whose demise I immediately set to work planning.

Sadly, my plans were sidetracked by the presence of Andrea, a red haired crackhead who decided to move in next door in order to be closer to me and Sue. The first thing she did was convince Sue to quit her job as a bartender in order to become a go-go dancer on Times Square. She then got her hooked on dope and seduced her into a lesbian relationship. I killed time jerking off to Glow reruns while Sue and Andrea kept busy licking each other's cunts next door.

One night, after driving a cab, I came home to discover three girls in my bed. As I looked at the zonked out Sue lying with Andrea and her scraggly girlfriend, all I wanted was some peace and quiet. After giving Andrea and her scrawny friend the boot, I proceeded to administer a severe tongue lashing to Sue's dolphin-like clit. The more I plunged my undulating tongue into her trembling twat, the louder her squeals became as I slurped away at her quivering clit, oozing fuck juice and sweat. Sue's thighs shuddered in ecstasy as my fingers slid up and down and my tongue thrust deeper into her gaping cunt, wrenching squeals of delight from her throat. I was slurping for my life. Sue paid half the rent and I couldn't afford to have her run off with a pair of dykes from New Jersey. My tongue burrowed deep into the soft pink crevice of her clit and my right middle finger slowly penetrated her anus, going all the way in, as she shuddered and twisted in a violent paroxysm, emitting squeals of pain I'd never heard. For two full hours, I shoved my penis down her throat and got her to come repeatedly by sucking and licking her clit. When it came time for me to take a piss, she opened her mouth and a hot stream splashed down her throat. She inhaled lines of dope as I crouched over her and allowed my bowels to empty a load of shit onto her back. I then smeared the soft brown excrement over and around and onto her two big breasts as she pulled me down onto my back and straddled my head with her legs. A shower of shit blasted out of her rectum onto my face as I opened my mouth to taste the warm oozing substance. I then violently vomited onto her face and licked the puke and shit up in order to gag and vomit again.

I felt totally clean. My insides were empty and covering the woman I loved. We rolled around and covered ourselves in vomit and shit and continued to lick each other's assholes until our tongues were sore. I snorted two bags of coke and puked all over a copy of the Good News Bible before passing out. When I awoke the next morning, the color TV and both VCRs were gone. Sue left a note saying she wouldn't be coming back.

So now I was sitting alone in this wreck, filled with vomit and shit, wondering what to do next. Why did she leave? Who did she leave me for? I didn't really care, but it gave me something to do with my mind as I lay there covered in shit. What a fool I am. A brainless fucking retard in a room alone. I just can't get along with anyone, I guess. Nobody's up to my standards. I made up this story by the way.

I don't know... I'm attracted to their beauty... elevated... It transcends the dullness in my life, but after a month of looking at them, I'm bored out of my mind. I don't want to know about their fingernail polish. I don't want to hear about what food they ate or what perfume they just bought. I don't need to see what clothes this girl just bought or what recipe she just found. I need to have my brain stimulated and all I can get is drivel. A useless stream of nothing perpetually for hours on end; the utter, unending boredom of living with a fool. There must be someone out there— a being with a functional brain who's half worth fucking. But who'd put up with an asshole like me? Forget it.

I'm trying to think of what I'm going to do next and I'm failing miserably. I don't give a shit. My whole world is falling apart and I just don't give a shit. Isn't that a laugh? How many years have I been trying to live in this stupid city, and for what? All my friends gave up and left like rats off a sinking ship and here I am alone in a room covered in shit, wondering what to do next. The world is in chaos outside my door. I'll try to forget the present. Remember the past.

At times like these, my mind wanders, pondering the misfortunes of even bigger fuckups than myself. It makes me feel better to think of how Tommy ruined his life.

Like the time he got so drunk in that bar uptown he didn't know what he was saying and three guys took a dislike to his presence. When one of them called him a fuckhead, he called the fat one a faggot. Out on the sidewalk, Tommy had his face beaten to a pulp by three drunken college students, landing him in the emergency ward of the very same hospital where he worked during the day, doing cancer research. The boot heels and pounding fists of the three drunk fucks fractured the cheekbones and split his right eyelid, necessitating reconstructive surgery.

In the process, doctors discovered four abscessed wisdom teeth, pulled them out and left the entire right side of his face numb for six months, a drooping eyelid and a few stitches the only visible evidence of his encounter with the academic community.

CHAPTER TEN

It took fifteen hours in a broken down van to get to Montreal, Quebec in order to show *Police State* and some other movies, only to have customs agents seize the films before I even got there.

I wouldn't recommend sending anything to Canada by Federal Express. Instead of delivering your package, they x-ray it at Federal Express headquarters and then send it to Montreal Customs, where a judge opens it and then views the contents, deciding whether anything in it is too obscene or immoral to be delivered. It is because of this that *Police State* and two hours of short films I made are now in the archives of the Canadian Police. Ironically, one of the things in the van that got through was a .45 caliber revolver used in a performance. I guess customs thought it was less dangerous than my movies.

All of my films were banned in Toronto last month. When I went up to show them at the Rivoli, a representative from the Censor Board closed down the show. Nazi Dick got away with showing his stuff there a week earlier because the censor wasn't tipped off by the kind of press coverage I got.

In the last five months, movie theaters in Berlin were attacked and partly destroyed by left wing political groups for showing pornographic films like Nazi Dick's. At Kinoeiszeit, ten enraged feminists broke into the projection booth and poured blue paint over the projectors that were showing *Fingered* and 1940's porno

films from Joe Coleman's collection. These insane fascists then broke into the box office and stole all the money before leaving.

Fortunately, here in America, places like the Collective and Millennium are dedicated to making sure things like that don't happen. They don't book our films.

"The old Puritanism says it's obscene; the new Puritanism says it's sexist. Step by step we advance further *and further into gobbledygook.*"—Robert Anton Wilson

CHAPTER ELEVEN

Some person calling himself Gore sent me a check in the mail for $50 to write something for *Phlegm Threat*. What could I do with fifty bucks? I could go out and buy five bags of dope, take a bus to Long Island and resell the shit to some fourth graders for $20 a hit. Who puts this thing out anyway? Rich commies? Trotskiite thugs? Everyone agrees that this magazine sucks, but what should we do about it? String up Gore and Seawood by the balls with barbed wire and flog them with copies of the Communist Manifesto? It's food for thought.

OK, so you've finally discovered there's something better to write about than how bad an actor Stallone is or what an embarrassment cliché-ridden movies like *Indiana Jones and the Temple of Doom* are. (Most popular video of the month—blecch!). After exposing myself to this imbecilic excuse for entertainment, I now know the true meaning of the word *fascist*. Films like this shove prefabricated notions of boring excitement at you in a non-stop orgy of stupid thrills designed to keep you from exercising any creative thought.

You are not encouraged to develop or solve problems by yourself. They are all invented and solved for you in a mosaic of violent bombast. Unlike real life, all the elements in this film are cartoon equivalents of good or evil, masking racist assumptions regarding the character traits of Asian people and sexist assumptions regarding the nature of women, demonstrated by the imbecilic antics of that suburban housewife buffoon who was masquerading as a lead actress, and the lame dialogue lifted from an old *Terry and the Pirates* comic stuck in the mouths of every character with slanted eyes.

Spielberg and Lucas think they can get away with all this regressive stereotyping of Germans, women and other foreigners by setting the whole thing back in World War II—which is supposed to make it safe—but it just doesn't work. No matter how hard they try, Lucas and Spielberg can't alter the fact that in the real world, forty years of systematic erosion of these regressive stereotypes has rendered them impotent to all but a few children like themselves. Just because we have a senile liar for a president doesn't mean we have to emulate his mentality.

Yes, underground films do exist, and as we who have been suppressed by the indifference of the bastards in the clouds are well aware, there have always been alternatives to the bubble gum of the mind peddled by Hollywood and Europe for our consumption. And for the time being, our capitol is New York. Ironically, as the center of our mass print media, the Big Apple vomits out more pretentious film magazines than anybody, but they're all written by narrow minded whores in starched shirts, so don't expect any coverage of the underground in the pages of *American Film, Film Comment,* or the *Village Voice.*

Underground films are only available by mail from New York. Since they are banned everywhere, they are almost never seen. Everyone is afraid to show them. The root of conservatism—fear of change—is a form of cowardice which afflicts nearly everyone now. But we don't care. We'll be laughing all the way to the bank ten years from now when the historians are sifting through this decade looking for something exciting. It's just a drag having to wait for them to catch up.

My cat has leprosy.

As I watch the roaches crawling in my bed, I'm wondering when I'll have enough money to finish the film I started over a year ago. That it should take me a year to finish a ten minute film due to lack of cash bespeaks the ignorance of a world which could vomit out diseased fungus like *Blue Velvet*. I suppose I should be grateful the air conditioning in the Waverly Twin Theaters drowned out most of the stupid dialogue in this lummox of a film. If this is avant-garde, then Pee Wee Herman is Rambo.

"O.K... so what's going on in New York, conceited, self-promoting transgressor?" you ask. At least five fatally overdosed fourth graders in Long Island paid me to give you the answer to this monumentally irrelevant question, so you better listen up, schmuck. I know it means more to you than it does to me since I've known about it for at least two weeks. We had a festival here designed to show off as many of these despised films as possible before the fire marshals could find out, and even though the whole shit wagon was put on by one of the slimiest assholes I've ever known—the late "Angel of Death"—I guess it deserves mention, especially since all the film mags turned up their noses at it, not entirely due to the stench of the Hag's lies, but to their own leprous hypocrisy. Forget that none of the filmmakers involved, three months later, have yet to receive one penny for their labors, at least it got us a centerfold in the *East Village Eyesore*, everyone's least favorite newspaper.

At the New York Film Festival Downtown, all of the boring and unclear films got the usual polite applause. Then they showed my film, *Kiss Me Goodbye*, and some people in the crowd began to produce hissing noises which pleased me, since to get any response other than polite applause from a group of art fags is a major accomplishment. I think part of the crowd hissed because they thought it was "sexist" or something, but I'm only guessing. When another film showed two dykes castrating a peeping tom, everybody applauded, showing what hypocrites they are. Afterwards, the director's girlfriend gave him an award for making it.

Jon Spencer of Pussy Galore caused the most controversy by showing *Pus*. Half the audience was screaming about how much they hated it, demanding it be taken off, while the other half screamed for it to be left on. Thanks to the retarded projectionist, the bulb blew out on the projector and when this happened, there were many happy cretin faces. Naturally, it was the best film.

Black Cat Tea, by Marzy Quazar, also elicited a chorus of boos and hisses from the crowd, simply because the girl who made and starred in it got bitten by a vampire played by Monte Cazazza. How shocking. By now the only clear indication that a film had any creative merit could be determined by the number of disparaging snorts it produced. By the same token, the more boring and aimless a film was, the more pleased applause it evoked from the snob crowd.

Tommy Traitor's trailer for *Where Evil Dwells*, based on the

Ricky Kassos Satan Teen Murders, was badly shot, sloppy and out of focus, distracting from the impact of the images which might have been interesting, especially "Baby" getting his eyes gouged out. I was especially amused at the naked girls strung up and the sight of Joe Coleman biting the heads off live mice. A bit like looking at a moving Bosch painting through a blurred kaleidoscope, the overall effect was annoying. Traitor got an award for it anyway. *Rat Trap* was mostly out of focus and sloppy, too.

I received my annual award for putting up with the late Hag's bullshit, half of a fifty cent candle. Next year it will probably be a piece of string. New York is now dead thanks to all the assholes who closed down all of the good clubs and ruined the ones still left. Blame it on the greedy landlords, pig cops and our corrupt mayor.

Tommy Traitor did a performance at the Cat Club and threw up onstage. Then he set himself on fire accidentally and fucked a skeleton while people trampled on the flames. I was a bit disappointed to hear the bouncers didn't give him their now obligatory beating-for-the-paid-talent, but you can't have everything. G.G. Allin went on stage, took a shit, threw it at the audience and got beat up by the bouncers before being thrown out onto the sidewalk in his jockstrap. The Catshithole then fired the geek responsible for booking these naughty acts. They should have fired the bouncers. The Evil Hag admitted, in her own words, that she was "a piece of shit" to me at her festival, promising to give me my print of *Totem of the Depraved* after a three year wait. A week later, she changed her mind proving what a liar she is. If I ever get it back, maybe it will be seen again, but then I probably won't want to show it. I shall title my book *Totem of the Depraved*. Why throw away a good title?

In 1986, the Cinema of Transgression provoked a viciously reactionary backlash from several surprising sources. Right-wing art rags like *CineAction, Snack* and *The Funnel Newsletter* became ventriloquist dummies for the movement by publishing articles attacking it, and played into the hands of the filmmakers they maligned by giving us more free bad publicity than we ever got from the *Voice*. (Fuck you, "Byron" Bruce La Bruce, fraudulent hypocritic.) Also playing into our hands by proving how narrow minded they are for not booking our films were the assholes at the Collective, ABC No Rio, Bleecker St. Cinema, the Kitchen, P.S.1., Millennium, the BFVF and the Funnel as expected. (All filmmakers should be warned to avoid ABC No Rio, whose director "The Weasel" has gained quite a reputation for stealing their door money and then lying about it.)

The rigidly conservative Robin Dickie at the Collective is now the movement's worst enemy, along with the useless Amy Taubin, "Ostrich" Hoberman, and Howard Travel Plan, all myopic fossils in need of retirement. Monkeys of a conservative age, the Ostrich Squad will be harshly judged by history for their cowardice and soundly forgotten when the time comes. Because of their exclu- sionary booking policies, many of New York's most important underground filmmakers have found themselves starving to death this year with no money to live on, let alone make films. The New York State Council on the Arts has also turned a deaf and dumb ear to our pleas for financial assistance to its eternal disgrace.

On the other hand, Tess Hughes Freeland in NY, Mark Shreier in Michigan, Debbie Shane in Boston, Steve Gallagher in Buffalo, Barry Stolz in Florida and Jon Killough in Ohio will all be remembered for their bad taste and courage in enabling a group

Zedd shooting "War Is Menstrual Envy" / Katrina Del Mar

of filmmakers whose work has been blackballed everywhere to at least be seen and talked about somewhere. While New York's curators and critics turned more reactionary than ever before this year, many friends were found outside our borders when California's *Rough Trade*, Ohio's *Alternative Press*, Atlanta's *Low Life*, Florida's *Suburban Relapse* and The Ann Arbor Film Festival all stood behind the Invisible Cinema in spite of massive indifference from entrenched quarters. It is they who should be remembered for not backing down to the forces of boredom and timidity the way everyone else did.

As filmmakers, we of the Cinema of Transgression must never forget we're at war with everything Hollywood and the established avant-garde stands for and it must now be obvious the latter will never forgive us for being a success outside the realm of their limited structures. Fuck them. As filmmakers, we should be commended for not giving up in the face of such total hatred from everyone in power. For continuing to make films in spite of the "alternative" power structure's total indifference, Tommy Traitor, Nazi Dick, Richard Klemann, Erotic Psyche, Michael Wolfe, Tessa Hughes Freeland, Jon Spencer, David Rutsala and others deserve all our support. They just keep making films while everyone else wallows in bullshit.

Festivals: All film festivals that charge "entry fees" are just scams to rip off filmmakers. All festivals should pay rental fees the night of the show to each filmmaker whose work is shown, out of the door money they collect. No filmmaker should be subjected to the indignity of having to wait weeks or months for a check to arrive in the mail. This insulting procedure should be discontinued—immediately by Todd Capitalist and the so-called Underground Film Festival—or else end the festival.

CHAPTER TWELVE

Andrea, the teenage crackhead who wanted to move in with me, was supposed to take me out to Tavern on the Green for a huge dinner. Instead, she went to Hotel 17 and died. They found a bunch of needles on the floor next to her.

A week later, somebody sent me a plane ticket to go to Sweden to read poetry at a big festival. European "culture" is all second hand, and occasionally people with money there pay people like me to bring them the real thing from America so they can decide what next to imitate. I spent the first night of the Poetry Festival in Goteborg bored out of my mind, wandering around a club while Swedish poets recited drivel to a well behaved crowd of Eurotrash. I couldn't get any vodka since all they had at the bar was wine so I kept telling myself, "Be happy you're in Europe," and looked for girls to pick up.

I kept noticing this one girl with a bald head with red veins painted on top. She kept stumbling and going to a sink backstage to pour water on her head. When the bathroom door was locked, she got mad and started kicking it and fell down on her ass laughing. I noticed her stomach and breasts showing through the tight dress she was wearing and also her big ass. I started following her in order to see if she'd get in a fight or fall down. She was far more interesting than the so-called talent onstage. She sat on a stool backstage undoing some bandages tied around her ankles and took her shoes off to massage her feet. She kept pouring beer on her bald dome because she was hot and this liquid soaked through her dress so I could easily assess the shape of her body. She didn't seem to notice anybody else in the room. I wanted to talk to her for some reason but I was too shy.

She had shaken my hand the night before and introduced herself in a kitchen belonging to the festival organizer while I sat talking to Dorota, a girl I'd been with eight months ago who was now pregnant. I just thought the bald girl was an ugly skinhead and ignored her. Earlier that night, she had asked me for a pen, which I lent her. She tripped and fell on the floor before she gave the pen back.

An incoherent video of Burroughs and Giorno was projected backstage. Dorota was standing next to me and I didn't want to be with her. Since she got pregnant, she seemed to age ten years and she never had anything to say. She just glared at everybody and wore black. Meanwhile, this bald girl in the tight wet dress kept getting looks of disapproval from everyone as she carried a chair around in order to get a better view of the screen. I kept staring at her, thinking she must be a mental case and wondered if I could say anything to her that wouldn't make me sound like an imbecile. She got up and asked me to not let anybody get her seat and walked off. I sat on a broken stool watching the seat in a room crowded with Swedish people. I sat there ten minutes and watched someone sit in her seat. She came back. I picked up my stool and told her she could sit on it, but she turned to leave. I asked her if she was leaving and she said yes.

I followed her and asked her name. She said her name was "Fritz" and she introduced me to her younger sister Doris, a bad Swedish poet in a tight green miniskirt and beret. I thought Doris was sexy, but she was too skinny and young and her poetry sucked. I wanted to heckle her when I saw her onstage but I felt sorry for her so I just walked away as she spoke of butterflies.

Fritz invited me to her apartment with Doris. I didn't know where I was, but I wanted to get away from Dorota. When we got to Fritz's apartment, I told her I was hungry so she said she'd make me food. She put cheese on a cracker and poured curry powder on it. She then got down on her knees and started scrubbing the kitchen floor. She spent an hour doing this and picking up cassette tapes and jewelry while her sister and I watched. I asked her why she was bothering to do this at three in the morning and she said her mother would beat her if she saw the place was a mess. Scrubbing the floors for no reason seemed neurotic and bizarre, but at least it was unexpected and she wasn't trying to impress me or test me. Then again, maybe this was a different kind of test. I ate some spaghetti and we went to her bedroom with her sister. There was a TV on with only one channel—the Special Olympics. I sat on the bed with Fritz and Doris and she said I could sleep in the kitchen. I said I wanted to sleep with her so she pulled a mattress out of her bedroom, put it in her mother's studio and told her sister to leave.

The walls were covered with elaborate collages of Marilyn Monroe, naked Africans, Prince and Hollywood starlets and her mattress was covered with twigs and leaves. I examined the round surfaces under her dress and got a hard on. I grabbed her ears and kissed her. I liked the way she smelled and the strange scent of an Indian perfume she wore. We made love on the bed on top of the annoying twigs while the TV showed an Olympic race with amputees. I laughed when one of the legless men fell off his wheeling device and had to be picked up.

They presented medals to the deformed athletes with close-ups of them crying. Fritz seemed nervous as we fucked, but she never said anything stupid or obvious. She sweated a lot and wore herself out. She ended up liking it but she acted kind of cold. She wouldn't look me in the eyes, but she brushed up against me with her head which I kissed. The next day, she told me she'd been raped by ten men and had lived two years in India with an Iranian prince who cut his penis off after she left him. Her real name was Frida. Fritz was an abbreviation of her first and last names. I called her Frida.

I went with her to the second night of the poetry festival which consisted of another five hours of milling around. The organizer, a middle-aged woman with too much makeup named Margot, gave me a bottle of vodka which I hid in the refrigerator backstage so I couldn't get drunk before I went on. This was a mistake. Somebody found the bottle and finished it while I did my "reading" to an indifferent crowd of apparent drunks. I was so distracted by the offstage talking that I ended up boring myself onstage. I didn't care about what I was reading and I didn't want to be there, but I was being paid $500 to do it. Nobody appeared to understand what I was saying and I couldn't speak Swedish. When the heckling started, I responded, "Go to hell, weasels!" and walked off. Nobody applauded. I hung around backstage for a few hours and wandered around the dingy cold club while boring Swedish poets whined academically at the polite audience. John Giorno told me about the time he passed out and awoke to find Andy Warhol giving him a blow job.

Suddenly, a girl appeared in a black dress holding a skinned dog's head. Her face was smeared in blood and her eyes were smothered in black mascara. Her hair was a rat's nest of black weeds and her makeup was sloppily covering her face in a

Brenda Bergman as "Buffy" in "Geek Maggot Bingo"

frightening clown-like grimace.

She asked Margot if she wanted to talk to the "friend" in her hand and Margot replied, "No, I've talked to enough dead things tonight." The vampire girl looked me directly in the eyes and said, "Will you kiss me?"

I was both repelled and attracted by the sight of her face smeared in blood. I stuck my tongue in her bloody mouth and we continued to kiss as people tried to look the other way. As our lips

touched and we stood in the middle of the crowd of milling cretins, I was suddenly swung across the room and felt the iron grip of Frida holding my arm.

She said, "Do you want to fuck her?"

I thought a moment.

"Sure, why not?"

Frida slapped me in the face and then stepped back to throw a bottle of whiskey at me. I ducked and it flew twelve feet, hitting Margot's husband, the co-organizer of the festival who looked directly at me. "I didn't throw it. She did," I said and stormed off. I didn't want to lose Frida, but she was mad so I decided to stay away from her until she cooled off. She had spent the earlier part of the evening putting white clown makeup all over the body of a beautiful fat Chinese girl. As part of a performance art farce, the naked girl lay on the floor under a twenty foot wooden tower while a dreadlocked bimbo cut the whole thing down with a chainsaw. This took an hour and a half. Any normal audience would have walked out on this but not these geeks. In their tolerance for everything, they revealed themselves to be utter fools. Frida returned and told me I could fuck the other girl. She then went to the toilet.

For some reason I thought I wanted to be alone with Dorota so I sneaked off to meet her outside. We walked toward the apartment I was staying at, but as she spoke of the baby carriage and the crib she wanted me to buy her, I started to realize that it was Frida I really wanted to be with. So I told Dorota I'd walk her home, using the excuse that I had to get an early train to Stockholm for the last two days of the festival. After dropping her off, I immediately took a cab back to the club to find Frida. I met her inside, a photographer took shots of us, and we left. I then took her to Eric's apartment and fucked her on the fire escape.

The next day, I went by train to Stockholm with a tall Swede named Johann and Diamanda Galas and her English twit entourage. When I got to the hotel in Stockholm, I went to my room, turned off the lights and went to bed. I wanted to wake up in three hours so I could go to the festival to see Nick Cave and Blixa Bargeld recite bad poetry.

My sleep turned into a nightmare as I felt a paralyzing force immobilize me. I had sensed this presence before, an unspeakable fear consuming me as if an alien mind was waiting to crush and destroy with the pure force of an unseen energy. I felt this force surround me and I responded the way I had by now learned to respond. I plunged into the essence of evil. "Go ahead, destroy me," I thought. I waited and felt paralyzing fear. I wanted to experience the next step—the dissolution of awareness, the force of evil overpowering me. But as usual, I woke up in a sweat. This force, which always seemed so real, had once again retreated when

confronted by my challenge. I was still afraid though as I lay there sweating.

Suddenly the door started pounding. I went and opened it. Dorota stood there asking to come in. I left the lights out and told her the dream. She told me she had taken the same hotel room as me and told me of a dream she had more than a year ago, before she had ever met me. She was pushing a baby carriage. The handle bar was missing one side. She then lost the baby carriage and entered a room with a man in a bed. She embraced him and said she then felt love for the first time. Dorota then asked me questions about Frida. When the questions got too personal I told her it was none of her business. I then examined her pregnant belly and felt the movement of the child within. She was nine months pregnant and I felt a neurotic kinship with the creature inside. She said it was mine. She'd also said two days earlier that if it had only been my child, she would have killed it, but since it was hers too, she was going to have it. I hated Dorota, but she was a beautiful Polish girl. In spite of the hideous emptiness in her brain, I found her compelling. We made love and lay in the dark so long I missed the entire first night of bad poets in Stockholm.

The second night Kathy Acker commenced a boring diatribe on the subject of cocks and clits delivered in a middle-aged school marm's voice which grated on my nerves. They stuck me on so late that most of the crowd had left.

I decided to tell stories off the top of my head and won over the audience before subjecting them to a film I'd made called *Whoregasm*.

I took a train to Lund and was met by a girl in a white mohawk named Boel who was putting me up there to show movies. I was also met by Frida, who picked up the heaviest bags I had and carried them for me. She continued to do this as we traveled throughout Europe. After I showed the movies that night, while Boel and Magnus ran bad super-8 films to a small crowd of serious Swedes in black, Frida and I kissed and held each other tight. I licked her eyelids and her ears and squeezed her before taking her to a bedroom upstairs where I could look at her magnificent body and fuck her. The next day I went alone to Frankfurt, Germany to show movies at Werkstadt Kino.

At the station, I immediately noticed the fat Nazi behind the information desk who insulted me in German after I asked him a few questions. I told him he was pigshit and left. The audience was tiny and indifferent at the screening and it rained the whole time I was there. The projectionist was a retarded idiot who continually tripped over the projectors and missed his change-over cues. Uwe Hamm, alias "Kim II Jung", let me stay at his ice cold flat with all the windows open. For some reason, Germans don't feel the need for heat and like to open windows when the temperature is thirty degrees out. I started to notice the peculiar phenomenon of middle-aged German housewives in pastel clothes pushing baby carriages while sporting Ziggy Stardust haircuts. During my whole stay in Germany, I didn't meet one girl. This pissed me off since I left Frida behind so I'd be free to find one.

Uwe drove me to the Stella Cinema in Northern Germany where they booked my films with the Blues Brothers movie. Once again, the projectionists appeared to be on drugs or lobotomized as the sound blasted a screeching fuzz out of the speakers and I was forced to hand hold a super-8 projector as it ran *Go to Hell* all over the wall. When my most overtly sexual film, *Whoregasm*, played, ninety out of the one hundred and ten people got out of their seats and left. The rest of the night, a gibbering seven foot cretin kept walking up to me to announce his wonderment at the audience's stupidity.

His breath reeking a hideous stench of booze, he lumbered about stating, "These films are fucking great...These Germans... are assholes."

He kept stumbling up to me to blither, "I-I-do-NOT-go-now-to-New-York."

"Good. We don't want you," I said.

He stuttered through a toxic cloud of alcoholic shit.

"You-You-are-great...These-underground-film-they-are-the-best."

"It's morons like you that make it all worth while," I said.

He listened intently, then paused with a look of confusion and despair, looked up in embarrassment and said, "I...go..."

I could now breathe again.

Uwe had promised a big blowout party to celebrate my first appearance in Germany. This consisted of me, Uwe and two squatters in an empty building standing by a table with pieces of bread and cheese. The building had no heat so I spent the twenty degree night lying on a bench with my clothes on, listening to trains pass by the drafty windows. "What a glamorous time I am having," I thought.

It rained the next day as Uwe and I drove back to Wiesbaden in time to meet his mother at the apartment. She was there to tell him he had to leave because it was costing her too much to keep him there. I know how he felt. I was being evicted from my own place in New York since I couldn't afford to pay the rent now that

ZEDD FROM THE FILM "WHOREGASM" / MARTA

Sue had gone to Hollywood to be a porno star. We spent twelve hours trying to get the equipment to work at his film school to do video transfers, but as usual, the German technicians were completely incompetent and nothing worked.

I took a train to Turin, Italy to show my films and met Marco Farano, a little Italian with glasses who took me to an old apartment by the station occupied by two guys named Mario. Italy at first struck me as dingy and depressing like the Communist Russia I had seen in movies, but I soon realized this was the most beautiful place I'd been to so far. The old buildings with iron spikes covering the windows and the near absence of the corrupting influence of American commercialism left this place untouched but a sadness permeated everything. The men were much less pig-like than I had been led to believe and everyone shared their food where I stayed and seemed to be infused with a natural affection—or at least mutual tolerance—and the presence of paranoia I was used to in New York was absent here. All the beds I slept in were soft and the soap had a different smell and I felt cleaner when I used it. I could tell these people were as poor as I was, but they weren't cheap, and they seemed to accept me.

Exhausted from traveling, I went to sleep in a room and awoke when Frida walked in. She'd been calling every place I'd been in Germany and Italy trying to track me down. She'd taken a train through Germany to get here and been detained by police several times due to her bizarre behavior combined with the Nazi-like dispositions of the conductors one has to contend with when traveling through Europe. They are constantly telling you to move to a different car for no reason. If I put my shoes up on an empty seat, it would enrage the conductors and even the nosy middle-aged passengers would curse at me in Italian for the apparently criminal offense of my posture. The spirit of Hitler and Mussolini are still alive in the minds of many bourgeois Italian scum and I had no idea how ingrained Italian sexism was until I was told how offended the people I was staying with were that I didn't keep a tighter rein on Frida.

She'd often challenge the Italians to a game of pool in a bar, which was an unheard of offense for a woman. These same hypocrites were said to be offended by the "sexism" of some of my films, or so I was told. "Why don't they blow it out their asses?" I thought. I bought Frida a wig before we went to Milan, where I showed movies in a tiny club jammed with irate anarchists

chanting football slogans and playing pool. An outraged girl screamed obscenities at me in Italian after the films ended so I held my middle finger up and repeated, "FUCK YOU." I think she understood. She spent the rest of the night trying to talk guys into beating me up but nobody would. As I sat next to Frida, holding a drink with my middle finger and smiling at the enraged Italian girl, I noticed a thin young lady with dreadlocks smiling at me. She walked up and started flirting while her girlfriend glared. Frida was also glaring as the girl held my hand and stood directly between my legs ignoring her.

Frida dumped her drink on the girl's head and told her to fuck off. The girl wiped the liquid off her face and stood there smiling. I pulled my hand back and crossed my arms, expecting a fight. The girl just kept smiling and walked off. Frida yelled at me, accusing me of wanting to fuck every girl I saw and asked if I'd be jealous if she did the same thing. She grabbed an Italian boy.

"Should I fuck him?"

"No. I didn't do anything. What are you yelling at me for?"

She sulked for fifteen minutes while I took tokes off a hash pipe being passed around, desperate to get high so I wouldn't have to think about the two Italian thugs that had been eyeing me ever since they saw me getting paid. We couldn't leave until the skinhead with a car, whose apartment we were staying at decided to go, and the vibes were getting worse as the night wore on. Naturally, it was raining outside.

Frida belched loudly several times as she gazed into a mirror over the bar, squeezing the zits on her forehead. She would constantly astonish people by pulling the black mane of hair off her head, revealing her baldness. She'd start sweating under the wig, so in order to soak it up, she'd get pieces of toilet paper and shove them under it. I'd start laughing when the toilet paper would slide down her forehead under the hair. She managed to make people nervous everywhere we went by walking up to them and touching them or interrupting strangers' conversations to ask questions in bad Italian. As I waited with Marco and his friend Gummo at a camera store, the manager and his wife were explaining features on the equipment. Frida walked up to the middle-aged lady behind the desk and grasped the necklace hanging from her neck.

"This is plastic, isn't it?" she said in Italian to the terrified woman.

Everytime Frida saw a person who appeared to be from the Middle East, she'd say, "Salaam a lai" to them, and half the time, their response would be an angry stare. She would then call them assholes. Every time she'd take a bath, the floor would be covered in water and when Marco and I walked with her through the streets, she'd leave us to talk to strangers. We'd then have to spend twenty minutes finding her.

Marco booked me for a final show in Italy at a squat in a fishing village called Imperia. Some guy named Roberto said he'd be waiting for us over the phone. On the train, Frida immediately stuck half her body out the window to feel the breeze as it traveled one hundred miles an hour. This made me and the other passengers nervous. They probably thought she'd fall out. I was worried about the one hundred dollar wig she was wearing getting blown off. I needed it for a "poetry" reading I was going to do in drag on Halloween. Frida was beginning to get on my nerves. Every time I'd try to read, she'd interrupt to point out a photo magazine or a church window. She couldn't stand to be ignored for more than ten seconds and as she hung halfway out the window feeling the breeze, I was hoping she'd fall out. She'd start moving bags from one shelf to the next, standing over people as they tried to read. I gave up trying, put my sunglasses on and attempted to sleep, ignoring her as she thrust pictures in my face. She kept opening the window and the compartment doors after I'd shut them just to annoy me and after I slammed the window shut and yelled at her for the fifteenth time, she ran out. She came back an hour later and woke me up to show me a meticulously detailed painting in a magazine of a funeral procession of ten hooded dwarfs carrying a dead Donald Duck wearing sunglasses.

She pointed to the dead duck's face and said to me, "That's you."

When we got to the station in Imperia, we took a taxi to the address Marco gave us. We walked up a flight of stairs and entered a tiny social club with a bar and a few teenagers trying to skateboard off some cardboard boxes. Nobody spoke English or knew who we were and I saw no posters announcing my movies. Roberto was out somewhere so we sat around while a couple of tattooed punks hit each other and wrestled on the floor and two guys tried skateboarding in the twelve foot space, constantly falling on their asses and laughing. I joked to Frida that I'd probably have to show movies in this room, never realizing that was their plan. A pot-bellied dwarf wearing a t-shirt walked in and mumbled that he was Roberto. He had a beard and looked like if you touched him, he'd break into a million pieces. He could barely speak English. I was supposed to show movies the night after tomorrow for two hundred and fifty dollars and he hadn't put up any posters or gotten any projectors yet. It looked like a disaster. I was in the middle of nowhere and I just wanted to go to bed.

Roberto showed us a room with no door and told us we could leave our bags there. We were in a squat run by lethargic anarchists and the tiny room with the bar was to be my movie theater. "Maybe they could find a bedsheet for a screen if they really got organized," I thought. I didn't feel like leaving all my clothes and films in this room that everybody was walking in and out of, so I had him take us to an apartment in town left empty by a Communist student. It was a small, one room apartment with a kitchen, a bed and a huge poster of Lenin on the wall, which Frida immediately covered with a sheet of paper. There was a piece of wood on the floor with six black roaches impaled with needles. They had been preserved by the student in some way and a strange odor came from their bodies.

I had severe misgivings about the organizational abilities of these lethargic Italians, but at least we had a nice apartment for

one night. I had dreaded sleeping on the floor with a dozen down and out punks and hippies. Not that I was any better than them, I'd just been awake for two days on a train and I wanted privacy. Frida made us an omelet and then we went to bed. She put on the wig and the sight of her Amazon body gave me an erection. The whole trip, I was constantly getting a hard-on looking at her. She'd stick her huge tongue out and wait for me to lick it—a disgusting procedure—then we'd start fucking again as the bedsprings creaked loudly into the night. I guess the landlady heard us because the next day we were told to leave.

Frida and I went for breakfast at a restaurant by the sea. We met Roberto and two punks carrying fliers announcing my films. The fliers said I was a TERRORIST and bore a crude drawing of a naked man wearing a goalie mask being crucified. This was sure to go over well with the police. They went off to look for projectors so Frida and I went to the beach. While an old French woman sat watching, Frida took her flowing white dress off and stood nude. She collected sea shells and rolled around in the water. The sight of her exquisitely shaped, nineteen year old body was astounding. She was incredibly beautiful. We lay on the sand and kissed. I could taste the salt water on her lips and lying on the sand under her young body, I felt free. The sun blanketed us in light as the waves rushed in and we shared life in an open world. No laws existed. No human intervention. The world seemed huge and I knew nature would outlast all of us.

That night, Frida got drunk and danced with the teenagers to punk tapes in a tiny room sticking her tongue out and grabbing every guy's crotch. Her dance was wildly obscene as she grabbed her breasts and shook them wantonly at everyone. She'd thrust her cunt in the faces of the laughing girls on the bed and do karate hits to the beat as her mane of black hair flew and a wild force was unleashed. We stumbled down the street toward the hotel I'd paid for across town. In the middle of town, where all the roads intersected, was a fountain. This was the central point of Imperia. Frida pulled the wig off, dunking her head into the water.

"Why don't you just get in?" I said drunkenly.

She immediately climbed into the fountain and immersed herself as the men across the square stopped and stared. She climbed onto the top of the fountain laughing, her voluptuous body showing through the soaking white dress and kicking water on the passing motorists gawking out of their cars in the middle of the square. I stood there amazed. This girl was completely free. She appeared to be nude. Frida was a force unchained, standing above us all, laughing and kicking water in our faces. I was so proud to be with her. She jumped down from the fountain and ran directly in front of a car, spreading her legs on its hood and rubbing her cunt. She stuck her tongue out at the man behind the wheel as his wife sat with her mouth open.

I took Frida by the arm and pulled her in the direction of the bridge leading to the hotel, hoping we could get a cab on the way, but none came. As we stumbled toward the bridge, she blurted that her mother had seen me with Dorota in Stockholm. She wanted to know if I'd fucked her. I thought a moment.

"Yes, so what? It didn't mean anything."

Frida exploded. We were now on the bridge overlooking a swamp one hundred feet below. Frida climbed onto the railing crying and got set to jump off.

At first I thought she was kidding, but then I saw she wasn't so I grabbed her and pulled her back. I tripped and fell onto the street and saw a car coming. I got up and it drove by. Then I looked behind me and saw Frida lying in the street waiting for a car to run over her. I picked her up and pushed her onto the sidewalk, lost my balance and walked into a telephone pole. It felt like someone hit me with a crowbar. Blood flowed from a gash in my forehead. Frida asked to see it and I pushed her away.

"Fucking cunt! Goddamm it, that hurt!"

We kept walking until we came to a park by the road with a swing set and sat down. I saw a car with a light coming and thought it was a cab so I ran into the street to stop it. It was a cop car.

The cops got out and started walking toward us.

"I thought you were a cab. You can keep going."

The cops asked us if we'd been drinking and if we'd jumped in the fountain.

"No. Do we look wet? We're just looking for a cab. Do you want to give us a ride?"

The cops told us to go home and left. Frida tripped over a chain fence and ran into the street. She laid in the street as cars approached from Imperia. I pulled her out of the street and we sat on the steps of an old mummified building facing the park. She started crying, saying she knew I wanted Dorota and all humans were the same. She hated humans she said. She had told me before of meeting a UFO and shaking hands with aliens in California. She didn't think humans were worth shit and she said she loved me but she didn't think I loved her. I told her that wasn't true and the only reason I fucked Dorota was because she walked into my hotel room while I was sleeping and got into bed with me while the lights were out. I told her I fucked her in my sleep.

Frida continued blubbering as another cop car pulled up in front of us. Two cops got out and started barking at us in Italian. They were rookies out to push people around. Somebody must have reported us. They looked at my passport and ordered us into the back seat of their car. The cop in the right seat pulled out a submachine gun and pointed it at Frida's tits. She started laughing as he barked angrily at her in Italian. I told Frida to stop laughing. It would only make them angrier and therefore more dangerous. I had visions of being mugged and raped on a back road by these uniformed mafiosos. They took us to the station where some fat cops tried to interrogate us in Italian. I told them they were maggots. They didn't understand. We sat there for four hours as they insulted and laughed at us in Italian. An ugly cop ordered us to empty our pockets on his desk. Frida opened the poster advertising the "Terrorist from New York".

"Why did you have to do that?" I said.

These cops were so stupid they never would have opened it, but now they carefully studied the document.

A cop finally showed up who could speak English. He said they'd have to take her to the hotel to see her passport. Frida protested that she didn't want to leave me because they might rape her.

"You don't understand. Italy is a republic now," he said.

How reassuring.

"Did you jump in the fountain?" he asked me.

"No, do I look wet? I'd like to know why we're here. We haven't done anything."

"Were you drinking tonight?"

"Yes," said Frida stupidly.

"Do you think maybe you drank too much?"

"No, I don't think so," I answered.

"Let me give you a bit of advice. From now on, drink fruit juice or milk. Alcohol is not good for you. Drink milk. Do you understand?" he said in a moralizing tone.

"What about beer?" I said pointing to the can of beer the cop behind him was drinking.

"No, that's private."

"You drink it. Why can't we?"

"No, no, that's private," he said, stupidly oblivious to the hypocrisy of his words.

When the cops left with Frida to check her passport, I sat on a bench as two ugly lady cops out of uniform sucked up to the cops behind their desks, asking questions about me. I knew that if I lay down on the bench I could get this one fat cop angry enough to get up so I did. He started barking orders at me to sit up and I just looked at him. He started cursing at me in Italian and got up.

"I knew I could make you get up, you fat pig."

The lady cops backed up against the wall terrified as the fat pig walked over, barking orders at me in Italian. Right before he got ready to hit me, I sat up.

"You're a fucking worm," I said as he screamed words at me in Italian.

By 5:00 a.m., Frida and I left the station, now aware of the police state that existed even here in this remote fishing village.

It felt good when I showed *Police State* the next night and a crowd of people applauded when my character shot a cop in the face. Two guys sat passed out in their chairs in another room while Frida taped cutout fish on their foreheads, stuffed garbage in their shirts, and lay dirty underwear on their heads. We left with a crowd

of people laughing at them. On the train through Milan toward West Berlin, Frida pulled the curtains shut and jumped on top of me as I lay on the bunk. She rode my erect cock like a horse as the train bounced up and down on our way to Germany.

We had to wait for a connecting train in the station in Milan and I had to use the toilet. I couldn't believe what passed for a public men's room in this place. Behind each door was a hole in the floor, no toilet paper and no seat. To top it off, some parasite sat behind a desk waiting to get paid every time someone walked out after taking a shit. He also sold napkins for people to wipe their asses with. I couldn't believe people tolerated this. Imagine paying somebody to take a shit! I went to the cafeteria and took a shit in a toilet without a seat and walked out, ignoring the lady behind the desk shouting at me to pay her as I left.

The cafeteria was the only place with seats in the station but you couldn't sit there unless you bought something so a couple dozen derelicts would buy coffee and leer at people all night. There were at least fifty empty seats in the place. An old woman sat down and didn't buy anything. Two cops showed up and ordered her to leave. She started shouting loudly at them in Italian. The only word I recognized was Mussolini but her impassioned speech denouncing the cops inspired my applause as they gave up and walked away. Unfortunately, she kept on shouting at everybody else in the room for another fifteen minutes and even when I sent Frida over to give her a picture of Marilyn, it only shut her up for a minute. Finally, the old windbag left and I could concentrate on the leering perverts eyeing Frida's exquisitely proportioned flesh as she argued with the bourgeois cashiers selling food. They were the kind of people who only smiled at you if they thought you had money.

Frida kept belching in my ear as I tried to sleep on the train to Berlin. The East German pigs rudely demanded identification from us, searched my bag and asked questions about my films. I threw leaflets announcing my screening out the window into the East German police state—as dismal a place as I've ever seen. The entire country was grey, no advertising was allowed and all the cars looked exactly the same; ugly boxes on wheels. Frida told me she was thrown out of a restaurant in Communist East Berlin for putting a napkin into an empty glass. I believe it. The small-minded fascists paraded about in their uniforms thinking their little suitcases meant something and every passenger on the train hated their guts.

When we got to West Berlin, we went straight to Doris' boyfriend Charlie's apartment. He was a skinny musician who spent hours over a computer he got the government to give him to compose music on. He insisted on keeping the door to his bedroom closed so no moisture could penetrate his delicate equipment. Frida immediately wrecked his kitchen cooking vats of food nobody ate. She'd fry potatoes, rice, salami and whatever else she could, lay out bowls of candy, bananas and cut up fruit—enough for a family of ten—and carry the mess into our bedroom. Three people couldn't possibly eat all the food she made, so it just sat there as we tried to move around it. An hour, later she'd start again.

One night when Charlie went out, Frida entered his bedroom and broke his dresser drawer. She spilled booze all over his carpet and spread her collages out on the floor. She cursed me in Swedish for trying to read instead of listening to her. I put the worst record I could find on the turntable and then put headphones on so I couldn't hear her screaming. She unplugged the record player and started calling me an asshole and a faggot. I hit her in the face and jumped on her back when she fell on the floor. I kicked her and went back to listen to another record. She glared at me awhile and then stuck her tongue in my mouth. We lay on the floor kissing. Then I went in the other room and watched T.V. Two chimpanzees in human clothes argued with each other in German. The monkey wife hit her husband over the head with a frying pan. This was the best program on German television. Charlie's apartment was ice cold and he kept the windows open, which I had to keep closing. His water heater took twelve hours to heat up before I could take a bath. After I took a bath, Frida got in the tub and covered her body with shaving cream. Charlie was in his bedroom trying to impress two polite German girls who had come over for a singing lesson.

"Charlie...Where's my razor!" shouted Frida.

"I don't know where your razor is, you bitch!" he shouted back.

"CHARLIEE! GIMME A RAZOR!!"

"I don't know where the razors are. Leave me alone!" he pleaded.

Frida got out of the tub and walked into Charlie's bedroom naked, as the two girls sat behind their cups of tea.

"CHARRLIEEE, YOU MOTHERFUCKER! GIMME A RAZOR!!" she screamed, "YOU ASSHOLE!!"

She came back into our bedroom putting some kind of white skin cream she'd stolen from a department store on her face. I laughed and told her to go yell at Charlie some more. The girls in the room weren't smiling, she said. Frida walked in again stark naked, her face and two tits covered in white goo.

"CHARLIE! I NEED A RAZOR!!"

"I told you I don't know where the razors are! Leave me alone!!"

"CHARLIEEE!!" she screamed. This insane fat bald girl was completely ruining the impression Charlie was trying to make on the girls.

"Get out of here, you bitch!" he cried in a pathetic squeal.

"CHARLIEEE, YOU BASTARD!! I'M TELLING MY SISTER WHO YOU'VE

BEEN FUCKING!!"

The girls sat staring at her.

"Get out of here, bitch! You're not telling Doris anything!"

"CHARLIEEE! YOU FAGGOT!!"

Frida enjoyed embarrassing people. I couldn't stop laughing.

"CHARLIEE! ASSHOLE! YOU'LL DIE FOR THIS!!"

"Get out! Get out!"

She came back in our room laughing.

That night we went across town to a nightclub Charlie recommended. The girls at the door wouldn't let us in since it was "Lesbian Night". This was Charlie's revenge.

Frida pointed at me. "It's alright. He's a faggot," she said.

"We don't care. He can't come in."

We went to another bar where Frida did her obscene dance all night and I got drunk. Charlie woke us at 7:00 a.m. and escorted us out of his apartment. When he said goodbye, Frida ignored him.

She belched in my ear all the way to Sweden. She dropped her wig stand on the floor of the dining car and a waiter picked it up and offered it to her even though we both had our hands so full we couldn't hold anything else. She shouted "NO!! NO!! NO!!" at him as he stood there holding the styrofoam head. All the waiters on the car now hated us. I told her there was no need for her to be rude to strangers. She screamed, "FUCK OFF!" She got me so mad I hit her twice and she cringed in the back of the dining car. Before we got done with our breakfast, she tried to go to the toilet. The waiters freaked out, thinking she was sneaking off and had the conductor throw us off the train. Frida desperately wanted attention at all costs. By being as loud, rude and obnoxious as she could, she hoped to taunt or bully me into hitting her. I tried to resist her, but when someone's been keeping you awake for three

Nick Zedd / C.M. Linabury

days acting like a spoiled brat screaming at you, you begin to wonder if violence is the only kind of communication that will satisfy them. In Frida's case, it always did.

When we got to Goteborg, Frida and I went to her apartment. She began making a casserole out of old pieces of pizza, beans, cheese, curry and rice. She put it in the oven overnight. She spent the afternoon putting cassette tapes in a box and putting sea shells in the bathroom sink. She picked up dirty laundry and took it downstairs and made more food that we never ate. The next day, she took the vat of slop out of the oven and added pancake batter to it, then put it back in. She made a pot of spaghetti we never ate. She was forbidden to enter her mother's studio so she got a knife and pried open the door and moved all her mother's paintings around. She took all her clothes off and jumped on her mother's bed, pounding it with a blanket so the twigs would come off. She'd lose her balance and fall down laughing. She repeated this procedure four times as I sat there laughing. She put on my pajamas and wore them in the streets, taking me to people's apartments and going into their kitchens to make food, then when people would wake up and see us, we'd get thrown out.

One morning, I got fed up waiting for her to make pancakes and left. Margot and Dorota conspired to get me "away" from Frida by making me dinner and showing me videotapes of myself at the poetry festival. This killed several hours while Frida ran all over town in my pajamas looking for me. She stole two bikes, repainted them in polka dots and rode all over town. The next time I saw her, she was covered in black soot from head to toe. This was because she tried to dye the stubble on her head with circus makeup and it ran all over her face. I washed her off in Margot's tub and returned to her apartment. She took the casserole out of the oven and added spaghetti to it. I took a bath. All my clothes were lying on the floor when I pulled the plug out of the tub. All the water leaked out on the floor soaking everything. I had to sit there for an hour, missing an appointment while Frida ran up and down to the laundry room drying clothes. She stole another bike and a pair of boots from a lady who lived next door to a business associate of mine named Mickie. Everyone in town seemed to hate Frida and all the friends I'd made told me not to bring "the frog" over.

When I spent one night with Dorota watching tapes at Margot's, Frida came by looking for me. Margot told her I wasn't there, I found out later. Obviously these people preferred to see me with Dorota whom they never liked before, but now adored since she was an expectant mother. I let them think they were manipulating me into getting back with Dorota in order to have a free dinner one night. They all wanted me to stay in Sweden to see

Dorota's baby get born, but I unfortunately had to get back to New York so I could do the poetry reading dressed like a woman for seventy five bucks.

Dorota tried to trick me into signing child support papers at the government office, but I refused and walked out. In New York, I was always broke and in Sweden, the government pays to support children. I played with Mickie's two and three year old daughters one night and wished I had a child of my own. Babysitting Frida for a month was enough to drive anyone crazy. I welcomed her insanity though. It was the purest freedom I had found, aside from that of Mickie's daughters. I regretted having to leave, but I was committed to wearing a dress in New York so I split.

On Halloween, four people showed up at Saint Mark's Church to see me read in drag. I got stuck in a cab in traffic behind the Halloween parade and arrived an hour late, but by then they had left. I didn't get paid. All the money I made in Europe was now spent. My landlord sent me a notice saying I owed him eighteen hundred dollars. I am now going to be evicted. In a matter of days, I will be living on the streets of New York. I wonder if I'll ever see Frida again.

CHAPTER THIRTEEN

They're selling condos on my block for one hundred and sixty-nine thousand dollars. I can't even come up with six hundred a month. I go to court again tomorrow. I'm stalling the eviction with one week adjournments and housing inspections, but as usual, there's no hope. I should be out on the street in a week. The squatters don't want me—they're kicking their own people out so they can expand their apartments. I wonder if rent is cheap in San Francisco. Maybe I should get Frida to pay our way out there if she ever gets to New York. Goddamn landlords.

I still haven't been able to raise the money for August's rent so I guess I'll be evicted. Since the "housing crisis" in New York has eliminated all affordable apartments, I will either be homeless or, if I'm lucky, I may be able to move in with squatters. Ten years ago, there were still a few apartments in Manhattan for people who weren't rich, but since the president cut the federal funds for housing and our corrupt mayor remains a puppet of the landlords who financed his election, I am unable to find an apartment I can afford. I've noticed most politicians bend over backwards to avoid taking extreme positions unless they favor the rich. I guess that way they figure they'll appeal to everyone. I hate moderates. They're cowards and hypocrites. How could anyone take a moderate position with regard to killing the innocent civilians in Central America? Especially when the bullets were paid for illegally by our "representatives" in the White House. The amount of insensitivity required to not even be capable of recognizing the injustice of hundreds of lives taken violently by force and deliberately destroyed, indicates a level of dehumanization that is quite appalling to me. But if an "extremist" assassinated the president, I would applaud him because all governments are run by criminals who belong in jail for the suffering their policies impose on millions of people every day.

CHAPTER FOURTEEN

In the midst of my approaching homelessness, I was invited to show a movie at a film festival on the West Side. As I sat dejectedly playing with a broom stick, Lung Leg appeared.

I couldn't believe it. I thought I'd never see her again. She'd been gone from New York for two years, living in Minnesota with her parents. She had a thin face and long stringy black hair. She was extremely beautiful. She told me of how her parents had threatened to throw her into a mental hospital because she had been seeing goblins running around the house. After being kicked out, she ended up living with some crack addicts and believed she was now brain damaged from smoking too much crack with Lilliputians. She had several hits of acid saved which she was planning to do on a special occasion. I wanted to ask her if this was the occasion because I couldn't believe the words that were coming out of her mouth.

She said she was now a sadist and was being tortured by a "communist war god-

Lung Leg / Clayton Patterson

dess" from Germany called "Ninny" who could change her form at will. Ninny was an insane fourteen year-old wearing a dress stained in piss, at other times a school teacher, Nazi official, thief, wolf, skeleton, or Medusa with two serpents coming out of her mouth. She would insult Lung in a whiny voice for being a "weak American" and planned to use genetics and "massive vampirism to destroy entire generations of Americans. Any sympathy toward the Germans is seen as weakness and will be taken advantage of." Lung told me that Ninny had scraped her vaginal walls so all her estrogen was now gone and she could never have sex. Ninny had made needle incisions in each of the vertebrae in her spine and injected liquid poison into her. Snakes emerged from her mouth and sometimes she turned people into skeletons.

Ninny was planning to destroy Christmas by turning it into a "German holiday" by sending empty boxes—signifying Communism—to all children. She wrote in her journal:

> They are using methods such as vampirization to suck strength from America. Any sympathy towards them will be considered weakness and will be used. They've used the idea of having German children with American women as a tactic to destroy us. The children can be used to take all positive attributes out of Americans— blood and family—afterwards killing the American and removing all American traits from the child in a racist technique. Removing sexuality from anyone who ate while Reagan was in power or benefited from Reagan money is considered to be a 'Reaganite' and will be destroyed. Or if your parents voted for Reagan.

She believed the U.S. government should be broadcasting witchcraft over the radio and TV so we could defend ourselves against the German mind invasion.

LEARN WITCHCRAFT AS FAST AS POSSIBLE IF YOU WISH TO SURVIVE... you ignorant Americans—is the message I am getting.

She told me she had channeled several spirits.

The actions, beliefs which strengthened the individual bring childhood from the bones of the individual.

Ninny could break people's skeletal systems and turn them into folding chairs—"collapsible structures," she said. She could reduce people into three steaming bones representing the three things they believed in, attached like a triangle.

Ninny could also turn people into radiators.

She showed me a diagram of a Jew on all fours whose spinal column had been ripped in two.

Jew becomes radiator to support and is steamed to death.

Human bodies were now being transformed into radiators, she explained.

I actually witnessed a massive vacuum that was being used to suck spiritual energy out of America into Germany. What they do with it when it gets there is very hard to tell. American memories are taken. They're taking any occult power they can find; any mediumship; dozens of people

*are being used. Effect: To destroy American children so
future generations will be insane; suffer.*

Was this all because German rockstar Blixa Bargeld had just
dumped her? Lung felt her mission was to remove all German
symbolism from American Christmas.

*Question: What are German things? Lamps, knic-knacks,
gingerbread cookies. Sucking the ripe fruit of the world
dry and leaving carcasses of a once great nation the
shreds of humanity barren..."*

Ripe fruit indeed.

She told me "the bigoted bitch" had been sucking her dry like
a vampire, breaking people's bones and reassembling them into
her face. Ninny made her weak and was destroying her life and
mine as well, interfering and preventing me from showing my films
in Berlin, she explained. I looked Lung in the eyes—her thin,
beautiful face showed she believed everything she was saying. I
realized she was completely insane. I kissed her long and hard,
holding her in my arms. We passionately kissed each other for
fifteen minutes by the bar. We went into the hall where they were
showing *Robert Mappelthorpe Getting His Left Nipple Pierced* and
we kissed and writhed about on the floor. She seemed horny
enough to me. Apparently Ninny hadn't scraped all the estrogen
out of Lung's cunt because we were as close as you can get to
fucking without doing it as we made out on the floor.

I took her to my apartment, walking through the meat district
at one a.m. where drag hookers stand on sidewalks covered in
blood from the slaughtered cattle that thousands of New Yorkers

eat daily. The sidewalks were caked with a lumpy residue in spots—obviously gore that had dripped off the dead cows. The whole area smelled like dried blood and dead flesh. In my apartment, Lung became childlike and wouldn't kiss me on the lips. We slept a few hours with our clothes on. I wanted to have sex with her but all the lust seemed to vanish when we found ourselves in bed together.

The next morning, feeling ugly, I asked, "How come we never fuck?"

"I guess it's because I'm a little girl now."

Lung used to sleep in a coffin when she was living in Harlem. Her roommate Charlotte ransacked her apartment and sold everything for drug money while she was out of town and then lost the place. Now Lung was staying in the apartment of an ex-girlfriend who hated me so much she wouldn't talk to me.

I took Lung out for breakfast at five p.m. and said goodbye as she went off to work—dancing naked for strange men in Queens.

CHAPTER FIFTEEN

Even though everyone told me I looked young, my age plunged me into a deep depression in which I contemplated suicide over my failure to be anything more than an unknown film-maker living in abject poverty in a city mutating into an upper-class shopping mall. All the cheap apartments were gone and soon there would be no more cheap hotels for me to live in. Plus, my last refuge—the company of young women—was starting to bore me. As I continued to brood and ingest information from books, my intellectual growth advanced far beyond the capacity of most nineteen year-olds and I found myself unable to relate to their problems.

While my age increased, my taste in women remained the same and every girl I ended up with was nineteen or twenty. This was fine at first and it was flattering to be considered younger than I actually was. Everything would go fine for the first week or two if I managed to space out our moments together to two or three intense bursts of fucking, but once I started talking to them, the seeds of disaster would be sown as their awareness of any cultural or political development before the last five years would be non-existent and my efforts to educate them would be met with zero interest.

As soon as I started talking about things I had experienced ten or twenty years ago, I started feeling like a redundant old man. They couldn't relate to what I was saying. Their world was too different. They had missed too much. In the last ten years, this country had become so bogus that the only cultural landmarks they could recall were laughably irrelevant and they all shared an equally lame and conservative taste in films and music, having never been exposed to anything more radical than a few generic thrash bands if they were lucky. In this alarming situation, I would find myself patiently trying to listen to their boring chatter while wondering how soon I would find myself looking for a new bed to sleep in.

I found myself alone most of the time, preferring the solitude of introspection to the paralyzing boredom of these girls' conversation. The more beautiful they were, the more stupid, and though I enjoyed the ecstasy of sexual release, without an intellectual camaraderie, I became bored.

But now that I was being faced with eviction, my immediate concern was to find a new girl to move in with. I had nowhere else to go. I had three days before the city marshals were scheduled to break the doors down and immediately started scouring the bars for young girls since I didn't have enough money to move into a hotel. I lucked out on my first try as I entered the bar on 7th and B at two a.m. and was invited to share a drink with a girl named Lisa. Three years ago, I had visited her apartment to buy dope and I'd once slept in Lisa's bed with her and Lung when I was getting over being dumped by Casandra.

Lisa was still trying to get her old boyfriend Sid back, but he couldn't care less as he now had another of his replaceable librarian girlfriends who all bore a strange resemblance to the thin bespectacled bartender. She was drunk and dejected—an easy prey—plus she was loaded with cash and after three drinks, I was able to overcome my aversions to her upper-class mannerisms and concentrate on the quality of her femininity. After a few sloppy kisses, she invited me uptown to be her roommate and since I had nowhere else left, I went along. As I entered her penthouse on 72nd Street, she flung forty dollars on the table.

"There's your spending money. Write a list of things you want and I'll buy them tomorrow."

I didn't want to push my luck too early so I skipped the list and concentrated on getting my clothes off so I could fuck her.

Considering the pressure I was now under, sex with Lisa was surprisingly easy. Being drunk helped. I was able to get a hard on with the help of Lisa's lips surrounding my cock and the sweet smell of her skin and the sight of her dark flowing hair turned me on enough to forget about what an essentially worthless human being she was. Right now this Mexican-Amercan girl was my meal ticket and it didn't hurt that she was lonely and semi-rich. She later told me I was the best lover she ever had. I wasn't sure whether to believe her or not. I just kept my fingers crossed and thanked my cock for being able to worm my way into her life.

Things went fine for two or three weeks. Lisa was easy enough to get along with as long as she had money. I'd get up early and run in Central Park, visit my acting agent who never got me any work and make long distance calls to business associates in order to set up a film tour of the West Coast in the spring. I left town for Christmas, visited my family and went to Boston to show films, staying there with an older woman for a week. I had made a good friend in this woman and I could talk to her about things that would never have entered Lisa's miniature mind. When I returned to New York, Lisa said she had missed me and it looked like smooth sailing for awhile. I wasn't paying any rent and I'd made enough cash showing movies in Boston to buy my own food so I didn't have to ask Lisa for any.

The first week we were together, she was giving me "spending money"—twenty bucks a shot. I could even get her to give me thirty or forty if I really tried, but now it was unnecessary. The only reason I was staying with her was because I had nowhere else to go. I never told her that, but as long as we had sex—which was never more than once a week—everything went fine. Lisa had entered a higher income bracket since getting a job "answering phones in a whorehouse" and was no longer the down and out junkie she had been three years ago when I'd met her. She was going to film school and writing a script, she said, but I never saw her write a single page of anything.

Things went fine, until the day something went wrong with her cable TV. Suddenly she could only get one channel and she immediately blamed me even though I hadn't touched her TV when she was out. Then she started misplacing things and accusing me of stealing, calling me a liar when I professed my innocence. Any time she'd insult me, I'd insult her right back, which was something she wasn't used to. I was ready to leave any time and I didn't intend to take any shit. I left town for a couple of days and when I came back, she was crying. She'd been fired from her job and had spent all her money on Christmas presents for all her rich friends. I was touched by her tears and the fact that she'd been fired for not buying her boss a sandwich when she'd taken a lunch break. I violently kissed her all over and thrust my cock into her moist vagina, keeping it there after I came. I lay on her with my cock inside. We slept together holding each other tight, my penis deep inside her body for four or five hours. When I awoke, we began to kiss and I got hard and we once more made love a final time as the sunlight filtered in the immaculate apartment.

RAY AND ANNIE SPRINKLE / KATRINA DEL MAR

I started buying food for us both and tried to clean up after myself as Lisa had insisted on maintaining an immaculate environment—an anal retentive affectation I'd always hated when exhibited by my mother years earlier. It was this fascism of superficiality, this tyranny of perfection with which both women had tried to imprison me. Lisa was now doing dope all the time, borrowing money from her rich friends and wallowing in the self-pity I thought she'd grown out of when she moved uptown. She started nagging me all the time if I left a sock under the bed or a book on the table, trying to destroy my ego by calling me a "house boy" and trying to get me to do dope runs for her, which I refused.

One night I went downtown to visit Nazi Dick, who years ago had been my greatest inspiration as a filmmaker. He was now selling his lease for $10,000 so he could continue living in San Francisco where he had been doing drugs for the last two years. Nazi was now a complete asshole, chomping psychedelic mushrooms and chain smoking pot and crack as he bragged about how much better California was since it had produced great men like Charlie Manson. Nazi had accomplished nothing in the two years he had spent there, aside from ingesting massive doses of speed and pot, and now insisted everyone should move there since—like him—we would all be doing dope if we stayed in New York.

I sat watching Lung, who appeared to be in a catatonic trance as Nazi Dick told me he consulted her on his every move. She had done so many mushrooms she was unable to speak and hid behind her hair until Nazi moved her into another room where she lay in a corner. A succession of pot customers, junkies and people like Gnatz, who compacted and disposed loads of garbage in the basement of a building he was being allowed to live in, wandered into Nazi Dick's place. We all started taking mushrooms while Nazi sat and watched his phone ring. Nazi's old girlfriend Robin arrived in a Mercedes and paid him back two hundred dollars which he left on the kitchen table, complaining that in California somebody would have taken it by now, but nobody would do it here. I picked up the wad of bills and said, "I'll take it."

He immediately got angry saying, "Don't do that."

I threw the two hundred dollars on the table.

"I don't need your money, Nazi."

Robin sat outside in her Mercedes honking the horn for an hour while waiting for Nazi to bring down some acid.

"I got the money. Fuck her," Nazi said.

Finally she left.

I called Lisa, hoping she'd come downtown to give me a ride after she copped. Nazi handed me twenty dollars for a cab.

"Now you don't need her," he said.

When Lisa called back to say she was coming, he told me to give the twenty dollars to Lung who was unconscious.

"Fuck that," I said. "Look at her. She wouldn't know what to do with it."

Lisa called from a pay phone on the corner and I went down to let her in. I saw her following a Puerto Rican dope dealer down the street. She was dressed in a mink stole with pearls and earrings and an expensive turban on her head.

"I'll be right there," she said as she walked away.

Disgusted, I went back up. When I told Nazi Dick what I saw, he went down to let her in. As he got there, the dope dealer was holding a knife to her throat, saying "Gimmie some money or I'll do a Marla Hansen on you." She gave him ten dollars. Then Nazi opened the door and said, "Here... Want some money?" and gave the guy twenty dollars. When they got upstairs, Lisa tried to pay Nazi Dick back, but he wouldn't take it. She handed me the twenty dollars to give to him.

"Here's the twenty dollars you wanted back," I said.

Nazi said he didn't want it so I pocketed it. Forty dollars in five minutes. Not bad.

Watching Nazi blow pot smoke in Lisa's face when she refused to take a toke, I got bored and convinced Gnatz and her to leave. Lisa said she'd take us to Beekman Towers, a swank bar overlooking the U.N. After the three of us got in a cab, Gnatz suddenly bolted out into the street. I guess he felt homesick for his garbage. Lisa and I sat at a table overlooking the skyscrapers of Manhattan and the East River, looking at our screwdrivers as a middle-aged pair sang outdated show tunes to a bunch of rich fucks in tuxedos. I drank half the screwdriver, got up and looked out the window realizing I'd left my press kit in a bag in Nazi's

Nick Zedd, Holly Woodlawn, and director Peter Strickland on the set of "Bubblegum" / Tessa Hughes Freeland

apartment. I went to a pay phone and called but there was no answer. Nazi was leaving town tomorrow and I had to go down to get it. I returned to the table and looked at my half empty glass of orange juice and vodka. I picked up the glass and walked to the far corner of the room, then pissed in it, walked back and placed it back on the table. "OK, let's go," I said as Lisa burst out laughing. The rich people looked at us strangely as we entered the elevator to return twenty stories below.

We took a cab downtown. Nazi wouldn't answer the phone or my voice as I stood outside his building with three other people who couldn't get in. Lisa handed me forty dollars and took a cab home as I went into a bar following a guy I knew. He bought me a drink. He then agreed to help lift me up to the fire escape hanging on the front of Nazi Dick's building. I climbed six stories, wondering if I'd be shot by one of the drug pushers who lived in the building as I scaled the metal steps past their windows at four a.m. Fortunately Nazi Dick's window didn't have any bars on it, but I still took my life in my hands climbing onto the one inch ledge pulling the glass down and sliding through the top. I would've felt really stupid if I'd fallen and died. I fell into the front room of his apartment and walked to the back where Nazi Dick was passed out on the bed with his clothes on. I couldn't believe I ever admired this man. The TV was still on and the phone was still ringing. I looked around for money, but I couldn't find any so I took my bag and left. I went back to the bar and tried to pick up a girl named Magenta who said she was a witch. When she asked me why I was talking to her, I said it was because I liked the shape of her ass, but she was only interested in teasing me and any other man she could find, so I left.

Lisa's nagging and her insecurities, compounded by the dope she was doing, were making her unbearable. When I didn't hear her ringing the doorbell, she burst into the bathroom screaming at me, calling me an asshole and ordering me to leave. As I packed my bags and proceeded to walk out, I was stopped in the stairwell by Lisa, who ran out in her underwear demanding her keys back.

"Not until I get all my stuff out."

She threatened to throw everything out after I left if I didn't give her the keys. I didn't know what to do. I didn't trust her and I had to go to work since it was New Year's Eve, the best night of the year to make money as a cab driver. Lisa was planning on going to a celebrity party to meet Eddie Murphy.

"Why'd you have to do this to me now?" I said, doing my best imitation of a basset hound.

"You know I didn't mean it," she said.

So I went back to the apartment and left my bag. I then left right away to go to work. At the end of the night, I'd made more than two hundred dollars. I returned to Lisa's apartment and found the door double-locked. She opened it and asked if I could stay somewhere else for awhile. A junkie mother sat on the bed with her three year-old daughter.

"She's in trouble and has to stay here. You can stay if you don't mind sleeping on the floor," she said.

"Thanks for giving me advance notice, bitch," I thought.

The only person I could think of who would let me stay with him now was Darren, the bass player from Nazi Dick's band. He said to come over when I called him so I packed my bag and left. I'd have to return later to get the rest of my stuff. Little did I know what a nightmare I was headed for.

Darren let me stay in his apartment on 121st Street and I slept for eight hours in an empty room. I then got up and took a train downtown to get the last of my shit out of Lisa's place. When she let me in, she demanded fifty dollars for long distance phone bills she hadn't received yet.

"Show me the bill," I said as I packed my bag.

She showed me one with a call to Sweden for twenty dollars. I gave it to her. The junkie mother lay in bed with the child under the covers. Lisa demanded more money.

"We'll talk about it outside," I said as I edged my way to the door.

In the hall, she demanded another ten.

"You're just a junkie desperate for dope money," I said.

"Send me the next phone bill if I really owe you anything."

She blocked my path.

"Gimmie ten bucks," she said.

"Here's your keys," I said, holding them out.

She wouldn't take them so I dropped them on the floor in front of her. As I turned to leave, she pulled out a can of mace and sprayed me directly in the eyes. I felt an instant stinging and a cinnamon smell as the spray hit. I closed my eyes and tried to back off, but she kept spraying it in my face and I realized I'd have to defend myself. I grappled with her, grabbing her wrists and pushing her across the hall. I hit her a couple of times and twisted her wrist and was able to wrench the can of poisonous spray out of her hand. I was ready to kick her in the head when she started to scream "Help! Help! Help! Help!" in an effort to get someone to come out into the hall so she could pretend I'd attacked her. I took the can of mace, grabbed my bag and walked through the exit door down the stairwell. All I wanted to do was get the fuck out. What she had hoped to accomplish by attacking me I couldn't understand. I only knew she was a complete asshole.

My face stung as I tried to wipe the poison off, hoping it didn't contain some kind of dye and ten minutes later after I got on a train going downtown, my eyes began to sting, filling with tears from the spray. I went to the emergency room of a hospital and had my eyes irrigated for thirty minutes and vowed to avoid that bitch for as long as I lived.

I was homeless. Darren said I could stay in his apartment uptown. He lived with his girlfriend Ingrid. Not wanting to jeopardize my living situation by getting involved with her, I started fucking an ex-skinhead girl who kept coming over named Gwen. These people were teetering on the edge of insanity. Darren was constantly being mugged by dope dealers when he'd go out to cop and whenever he'd return, Ingrid would be sitting in my bedroom talking to me. They'd have jealous quarrels over this, even though nothing was going on. One night Gwen started hitting me and had to be restrained by Darren and Ingrid because I didn't laugh at one of her bad jokes. She wanted me to beat her up and tried to provoke me into a fist fight but all I did was deflect her kicks and punches. For this I was called a faggot.

Getting tired of this shit, I got a room at Hotel 17, a decrepit mausoleum for welfare winos, soon-to-be-dead junkies and would-be heavy metal stars. Two doors down from my room, a fat man in horn-rimmed glasses and a World War II flak jacket would play warped Johnny Mathis records and scream, "FUCKIN GODDAMN SHITEATING MAGGOTS! I'LL KILL THE NIGGERS!"

When a Buddhist next door started chanting, "Namyo ho renge

NICK ZEDD AND KEMBRA PFAHLER FROM THE FILM "WAR IS MENSTRUAL ENVY" / KATRINA DEL MAR

kyo" to herself for an hour every morning, I'd blast rap tapes. To get even, she'd pound on the walls blasting her radio and the slob in the flak jacket would scream.

"GODDAMN MOTHER FUCKING FAGGOTS!! I'LL KILL YOU!! SHUT THAT SHIT OFF!!"

Down the hall, a four hundred pound hag would be visited daily by a toothless wino with no shirt on, reeking of booze. After two minutes the hag would scream, "GET OUT! GET OUT! YOU SHITHEAD!" and he'd stumble into the hall to look for his room.

My ex-girlfriend Sue called from LA. She gave up being a porno star after her yuppie boyfriend kicked her out of their apartment. She returned to New York to live on the second floor of Hotel 17, inhaling one hundred dollars worth of dope daily, in between doing peep shows on Times Square and nodding out in front of a TV set I gave her. I started making money writing porno stories and got a job acting in Kembra Squalor's super-8 movie *Trilogy of Teri* with Annie Sprinkle. In this film, I was required to wear a dress, lipstick and makeup, and did a scene where I pissed on a girl's legs. Before doing the scene, I was given a pill that turned my piss fluorescent orange. I then modeled in the nude for Annie's camera and appeared in *Adam* and *All Male* magazine in leather pants with a naked girl. It was the first time I'd ever been paid to jerk off.

I then played the lead role in a science fiction movie directed by a woman named Malice. In this movie, I played a lawyer in the future who, after getting disbarred, discovers a genocidal plot by the scientists of a corporate dictatorship that's gentrifying the entire planet. I was involved in a "love triangle" in the film with two female characters. I brought along a girl who got us a limo ride to the shoot and fucked her under the sound stage while the cameras rolled on the lead actress and another guy.

Any girl who was fat I was immediately interested in and I kept looking for fat girls all summer. Sue was too busy nodding out in front of the TV to notice. Sometimes I would fuck three girls a day, going from one apartment to the next, trying to figure out which one I liked best. For some reason I always kept coming back to Sue. Why, I don't know. She certainly wasn't as fat as some of the girls I'd been with. Maybe it was her round face or the way she tied her hair back. Or maybe it was just that she lived on the second floor.

When she'd fall asleep with her mouth open, I could see her tongue twitching inside which would drive me crazy. Once I saw some spit dribble down the side of her mouth like a baby and I got so hard I had to stick my tongue in. Closing her lips, she sucked on my tongue in her sleep as I moved on top getting into position. I gently rubbed my erect cock up and down over her smooth shaved pussy until it became moist. I removed my tongue from her mouth and licked her delicate eyelids as she slept, unaware of the lust she was igniting. A moan emerged from her lips as I entered her soft pink crevice and gently moved my cock slowly forward into her tight wet interior. The sight of her tongue gently undulating beneath her lips continued to excite me as I pushed my cock in and out of her pussy and moved my fingers over her round smooth stomach up to her milky white tits. As my fingers squeezed her erect nipples, she started to moan. Clutching her hair—tied back with a pink bow—I gently pulled with my left hand, making her face move up and her eyes flutter open. I stuck my tongue in her mouth and rotated it around hers, then licked her lips and pumped my cock deep inside her trembling vagina.

The room was pitch-black except for the light coming from a television with the sound off. An actress playing a Civil War widow

SUSAN MANSON AND NICK ZEDD

was crying and the sight of her tears excited me. I imagined I was making love to her. Turned on by the sight of her buttoned-up collar and tied back hair, the lacy fabric of her dress and her Victorian conservatism, but mostly by the look of fear in her face, of crushing defeat and abject humiliation, sorrow and loss, the beauty of her vulnerability and the depth of her love, I transferred my lust for this woman to Sue, whose fragile beauty possessed a quality of perfection to me. I imagined I was an enemy soldier and was now going to rape a helpless widow with tears in her eyes. Had she been on the battlefield where a thousand men died? Had she seen the bleeding bodies blown to pieces, the severed arms and legs twitching in the dirt or the jagged bones sticking out of the torn smoking flesh of men who were not yet dead? All she knew was the pain of loss and the terror of her loneliness. But her pain which excited me so, would now be surpassed by the terror of this violation as I plunged my cock over and over into her trembling pussy and relived a rape from a hundred years ago.

As I traveled through time, a spirit of evil inhabiting my brain, I felt the liquid rush of eternity pulverizing the good, the innocent and the ignorant over and over again. This was my dream and I was ready for it any time Sue would pass out, her open mouth waiting to be filled, her open cunt waiting to be fucked, her open throat waiting to be squeezed by the force of death inhabiting me.

As I came inside her, an explosion of lust destroyed all boundaries propelling me out into space beyond good and evil; beyond the human race and all its concerns and illusions to an awareness of the Void. The one which awaits us all. The Void: awaiting you when you look death square in the face and just don't give a fuck.

CHAPTER SIXTEEN

March 1990: My second tour of Germany.

If it weren't for the money, I wouldn't be here. Germany is a timid and feeble nation that looks to America for all its trash. These Krauts were boring the shit out of me when they weren't stumbling over their projectors. I started this fucking

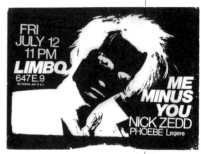

tour in Frankfurt. I then showed movies in Stuttgart in an old subway.

With no hope of excitement, my "tour guide" Uwe and I drove to Nuernberg. Standing in the projection booth of the Kino Im Komm, moments before the show was to begin, I looked into the theater and saw a bunch of people in ski masks blowing whistles. A gang of radical feminists had broken in and were throwing garbage and catshit all over the audience. The feminists threw manifestos on the floor claiming they were responding to the "chauvinist reactionary provocation" of the program notes announcing my films. They threw acid on the screen. Then they ran out. Nobody in the audience left.

Looking at the trash filled theater, I told the crowd, "I don't think the feminists are environmentalists."

Then the films played. Thanks to the feminazis, I got on the front page of the paper the next day.

Later that night in a bar, somebody shot tear gas off to protest my presence and cleared out the place. This was the excitement I was hoping for. Then in the lobby of the apartment building where I was staying, a middle aged German man attacked and attempted to strangle the guy I was staying with. He didn't like the way I looked. He later called the cops and after they left, came up to gloat at us and point his finger in our faces. I hit him and kicked him down the stairs. He called the cops again and when they showed up, I had to show them my passport before they would leave.

After Berlin and Hamburg, I planned to go to Sweden and do one more show, but the trip was ruined when the police in Denmark woke me up at four in the morning and escorted me off the train. They told me I wasn't welcome in their country and sent me back to Germany for being a "non-Nordic alien". They threw a black guy off the train for the same reason. I kept asking the cops why they didn't want me in their country and they kept saying I might look

for a job there. I had to pay my own ticket back, so I wasted four hundred marks for nothing. Europe can be trying. There's too many rules and most of the people are ugly. People in New York are ugly too, but they mind their own business more.

After Sue returned to New York, she resumed her flirtation with chemical dependency, spending hours staring at a television set while allowing our apartment to mutate into a stinking pile of garbage. In the summer of 1991, she could be seen wandering around Stanton Street, holding open cans of cat food, calling out the names of her adopted stray cats whom she'd spend hours talking baby talk to before nodding out. Many of the cats she'd take in would be sick and would vomit and spray spunk all over our apartment. Her favorite, Puke, would regularly shit and vomit on the bed and in the bath tub, but Sue resolutely resisted taking him to a vet, preferring to invest her money in narcotics. In August of 1992, after she left me, Sue gave birth to a son, Augustus, who she promptly left with her mother in New Jersey before returning to her career as a go-go dancer on Times Square where she can be seen seven nights a week, three hundred and sixty-five days a year entertaining lowlifes.

CHAPTER SEVENTEEN

I have been asked to say a few words on behalf of the late G.G. Allin, an individual I once knew but never took very seriously. For those too square to know, G.G. was a singer in a series of punk bands that never made it big. He was on the verge of becoming famous before he died of an overdose. I don't think his life particularly deserves a eulogy and if he were here, he'd probably tell us all to fuck off. Having witnessed more than a few of his celebrated performance pieces and successfully eluded the flying turds of this warrior poet, I can now pass judgment on his barbaric antics. Perhaps those of you less familiar with Mr. Allin's oeuvres are looking to me for an opinion upon which to base a consensus. Think for yourselves, assholes.

Far be it for me to speak unkindly of the dead, but as far as I'm concerned, G.G. was a fool. Since he's not here to defend himself, I don't feel too good about saying bad things about him, but the same thing will probably happen to me once I'm gone, and in a way, G.G.'s death serves as a challenge for all of us to face the truth, which I've always tried to do anyway.

G.G. went out of his way to be hated. He spread hatred and stupidity everywhere he could. One theory advanced for his psychopathology was a childhood of sexual abuse. Who knows? Furthermore, who cares? I consider it a joke that I'm even writing about him. His minimal talents were focused on a crude form of infantile self-promotion manifested in public filthiness.

Allin was an overgrown kid who believed passionately in some kind of twisted rock n' roll myth wherein he could run roughshod over everyone else's feelings and rights in order to exalt his status as a shit-covered asshole at "war" with the underground. His understanding of the politics of confrontation and the aesthetics of late twentieth century dadaism was limited, anti-intellectual, and ultimately boring. I was too bored with him to bother attending any of his last few gigs. I am not a masochist. I never would enjoy being picked out of a crowd and assaulted by a fat, nude punk rocker covered in his own shit. Maybe some people do. Some of you might deserve to be assaulted for being jaded, cynical voyeurs looking for a spectacle to turn your noses up at. In every crowd, there's someone who deserves every drop of saliva and excrement that can be thrown on him. I myself, when I did go, would place myself directly behind the recording equipment and technicians taping the proceedings, hoping that Allin would avoid injuring anything near it since he considered the preservation of his sound and image so important to posterity.

I was never afraid of G.G. It was myself I questioned when in his presence. He had a way of testing your limits by being willing to go to whatever extreme there was to prove his manhood, his fearlessness and his willingness to do that which would be considered "outrageous" or "shocking" to his parents. He once proposed that I shoot a film of him killing someone. We were to rent a hotel room and go out looking for a suitable victim. He would then kill the person while I filmed. I was initially interested but the chance never presented itself when he failed to turn up at the hotel I was living in. I was relieved. I didn't really want to be an accessory to murder. Like his pledge to commit suicide on stage, unrealized due to a convenient arrest and prison sentence for assault lasting two years, many of G.G.'s more outlandish claims were nothing more than flatulence.

One Sunday afternoon I followed him with a video camera around Boston hoping he'd do something interesting. After kicking in a car window and blowing up a TV, G.G. inhaled a paper bag full of White-Out. I was let down. Nobody died. Later, G.G. half-heartedly attempted to undress and rape a girl who mistakenly walked into a room full of punk rockers and lowlifes like myself. I was the one person in a room full of seven who pulled G.G.'s arm off the girl and told him to let her go, which he did with no resistance. I don't think G.G. really wanted to rape the girl. What he wanted was to test us—to see how far we would let him go before stopping him. In this way he forced me to look at myself and recognize the limits I'd place on my own freedom. I could have joined in a gang bang like any other cromagnon, but my own self respect and the pleading look in the girl's eyes wouldn't let me.

Naturally, the media belatedly zeroed in on the latent enter-tainment value of this overgrown baby who would shit on himself and his audience. The media loves to spotlight people like Louis Farrakhan, Oliver North and David Berkowitz for the same reason; they all have so little credibility. But then neither does the President, Jerry Rivers (a.k.a. "Geraldo"), the F.B.I., Congress, Dan Rather, or most of the hundreds of venal celebrities we encounter over the airwaves. Michael Jackson probably ruined more young boys' lives than G.G. ever could. G.G.'s spectacle was real though. Michael Jackson and Madonna's are fake. Even though he cried wolf and never got around to shooting himself in public, G.G. as a performer had more integrity on a barbarian level than any of the posing frauds on MTV. Not that it merits praise, the world is too full of idiot hate and mindless brutality as it is. What we have always needed is more love, more compassion, and more friend-

G.G. ALLIN'S SKULL FUCK [3]

by NICK ZEDD

MAY 5:
I WENT TO BOSTON THIS WEEKEND FOR A "READING" WITH G.G. ALLIN. I PUNCHED OUT A HECKLER IN THE AUDIENCE AND GOT IN A FIST FIGHT WITH FOUR POETRY FUCKS.

G.G. BROKE A WHISKEY BOTTLE OVER HIS HEAD, TRIED TO RAPE A GIRL IN THE AUDIENCE AND GOT BEAT UP BY TWO GUYS.

HE PUT HIS HEAD THRU A WINDOW, LIT A NEWSPAPER ON FIRE, THREW CHAIRS AT THE AUDIENCE AND CUT HIMSELF UP WITH A BROKEN BEER CAN BEFORE BREAKING THE MIKE.
THEN HE LEFT.

G.G. WANTED TO MAKE A SNUFF MOVIE WITH ME THE NEXT DAY BUT I COULDN'T EVEN GET HIM TO PULL HIS PANTS DOWN AND DO HIS "BALL DANCE" ON VIDEO. HE KICKED OUT THE WINDOW OF SOMEONE'S CAR AND TRIED TO RAPE A GIRL IN THE APT. WHERE WE WERE TAPING, BUT I FELT SORRY FOR HER SO WE LET HER GO. WE COULDN'T FIND ANYBODY TO KILL SO WE JUST LISTENED TO RAW POWER AND G.G. INHALED A PAPER BAG FULL OF WHITE OUT.

G. G. ALLIN FLYER BY NICK ZEDD

ship—not to mention cash—all values G.G. opposed just as Bill Clinton and Janet Reno did when they immolated seventy-six Christians in Waco, Texas. Clinton is a baby burner. G.G. atrocities pale in comparison.

The number of civilians murdered by U.S. troops in Somalia, blasting lead into crowds of innocent people, was a direct result of decisions made by individuals in the highest levels of our government—people who are daily held up for admiration by a media that thrives on hypocrisy and lies.

To demonize clowns like G.G. Allin serves the interests of the ruling class which dictates the media agenda, always looking for a distraction from any useful organizational opposition to its pervasive control. A genuine, though misguided rebel like G.G., as motivated by sheer self promotion as he was, in some way exposed us to the essentially empty nature of what the media thought was important.

One night, a week before he died, G.G. threw a beer mug across a bar and hit a dancing yuppie in the face, drawing blood. It was an idiot act that served no purpose and had no point. G.G.'s final retribution came from his own hands, by accident, of a heroin overdose. A cowardly death, typical, predictable and disappointing to anyone dumb enough to have believed in him. One of his bands was called The Disappointments. Earlier that day in his last performance, G.G. punched out a heckler, took a shit and smeared it all over his nude body, then chased his audience out of the converted gas station on Avenue B, as the plug got pulled on his band. He then ran into the street nude and blocked a bus full of people before stumbling away and hanging onto a lamp post. He vanished as several cop cars arrived, blocking traffic and causing a chaos far worse than his brief performance. The spectacle of a squad of cop cars blocking four lanes of traffic in response to a club manager's complaint over his act, like the one I witnessed a year before on Third Avenue, was G.G.'s greatest accomplishment. He altered daily life. It was a minor achievement, though a stupid one. By throwing shit on a fleeing audience, and with the help of New York's Finest who failed to catch him, G.G. managed to cause a tie-up that inconvenienced hundreds of strangers who didn't even pay to see him, spreading a little more hate and confusion in a world that would never appreciate it.

I once asked G.G. why he dedicated his life to such a selfless mission, injuring and poisoning himself to the point of hospital-ization to simply entertain a few hundred strangers. He couldn't say. He was an imbecile. He insisted he hated everyone and didn't care about his audiences, but in reality, he cared deeply, far more deeply than they deserved. He really thought his audiences merited his hate—a hatred so misdirected it always ended up hurting himself more than it did the spectators looking for a cheap thrill. He reminded me of a would-be Hitler—a fucked up little misanthrope who'd destroy the world if he ever got any power for no reason except his own inferiority complex which needed compensation through mindless acts of violence.

G.G. was a danger to himself and others and ultimately a failure on any artistic level. But as Robert Williams has said, "If it commands attention, it's culture. If it matches the couch, it's art." As a counter cultural icon of mindless barbarism, he stands alone. Few sociopaths have gravitated to musical entertainment as a realm for self expression until recently. With the popularity of rappers like Tupac Shakur who makes videos extolling respect for women and then participates in a gang rape in his hotel room, one starts to miss the mongoloid charm of G.G. who once recorded a tune called "Expose Yourself to Kids". Michael Jackson would tearfully lie about his acts to the world in much the same way his parents did, the Age of Denial in full effect.

G.G. always was what he claimed to be—an animal—a sick, worthless piece of shit, Jesus Christ and Satan. His biggest flaw was his inability to see anything better in anyone else—to recognize something unique and beautiful in others—in short, to transcend himself, the ultimate act of transgression by which one stops being a victim or victimizer. To love is the most revolutionary act, for it brings us outside of ourselves. To turn yourself inside out is the hardest thing to do in a world of corruption and pain, betrayal and lies. It involves an act of faith in yourself that few of us get a chance to do nowadays.

Maybe G.G. experienced this. But his whole life was dedicated to making us think he didn't.

CHAPTER EIGHTEEN

I spent my last full day in New York working as a P.A. on an MTV video, pushing a broom and carrying lighting equipment in a warehouse with no air conditioning in 100 degree heat. I was told not to sit down or drink for fifteen hours or I would be guilty of "not pitching in". The only good part was when the "director" asked me to shoot some inserts on a Super-8 camera. Nobody introduced me to Beavis and Butthead.

A day later, I took a plane to Sweden. Having lost my apartment, girlfriend, and work prints of my last three films a few months before, I decided to leave the country before my luck ran out. After eleven hours, my flight from New York to Goteborg was over. As I walked toward the exit with my bags, I was pulled aside by two customs pigs who made me open all my luggage so they could look for drugs.

"What do you think of drugs?" they asked.

"Drugs are nice," I responded.

I was told to go to a room where I was strip-searched and made to wait two hours while the police looked at my movies. Whenever I'd try to leave, I would be told by the cops to go back and wait.

Finally, I asked, "Why am I being detained?"

I was informed by a cop that my films were "sick" because somebody was cutting himself in *War Is Menstrual Envy*.

"We don't want people in Sweden to imitate this kind of perverted behavior. We are not sure you should be allowed into the country."

"They're only movies," I muttered.

There was much heated discussion and many phone calls were made by the cops in other rooms. I slouched on a wooden bench for an hour, trying to figure out how to get into the country without losing my films. If I let them cut out the part with Oddo slicing himself with a razor, maybe they'd let me in, I thought. Should I just let them keep the prints? I'd already had to stage a benefit in New York to raise fifteen hundred dollars to get them reprinted after a cab driver drove off with them in his trunk. Was it worth losing them again to finally meet my four year old son Kajtek whom the police in Denmark stopped me from seeing in 1990 by deporting me from the country before I could get to Sweden for no reason other than, "You might look for a job in Copenhagen?" Was there some higher force conspiring to destroy me everywhere I went? No, I decided I had to get in. Fate had to finally be on my side after so much bad luck. I had spent most of my money to get here. I would call the American consulate and protest any decision to prevent my entry and get myself arrested if necessary since the pigs had no right to keep me out.

I said I had to go to the toilet and was escorted by a cop who asked, as I was taking a shit, "Narcotics?"

"No thanks," I replied.

He then checked the toilet for drugs. I was returned to my cell for thirty minutes. Then another pig came and asked how many movies I brought and how much money I planned to make selling them. I was once again informed that my movies were "sick" and asked if the cutting was real.

"It's just special effects like in Hollywood."

They looked at me suspiciously.

"What I'd like to know is which one of you cops is a qualified art critic?"

They couldn't give me an answer. They didn't understand the question. They were very concerned that the person cutting himself in the film was bleeding. Finally, they decided to let me go.

As I was packing my bags, a lady cop asked me, "How real is your film?"

"As real as you want it to be."

She said, "I don't want it to be real. Do you want it to be real?"

"No comment," I replied.

"Do you do drugs?"

After a long pause I answered, "If I did, I wouldn't tell you."

She held up my book.

"You call this art?"

"Other people do."

"I call it SICK."

"You're a COP, not an ART CRITIC."

Finally, I walked out and met my son, his mother and Mickie in the lounge. Later that day I noticed the one object the police decided to confiscate—a can of shaving gel.

CHAPTER NINETEEN

Five days after getting into the country, I was asleep in bed, lying next to Dorota. Someone knocked on the door. I heard Kajtek talking to some men in the hall. Kajtek let three cops in. They stood and watched while I got dressed and told me they wanted to talk to me at the police station. I asked one cop if he had a search warrant and he said he didn't need one since we were in Sweden. They grabbed all my video tapes and the backpack holding all my movies while I called the American consulate and got put on hold.

Kajtek started crying and told them, "Leave my daddy alone or I'll kick you."

When the cop started walking out with all my films I told him, "You can't just take my possessions like that. You don't have a right to do that."

"I have the right."

"No you don't and I'm not giving you permission to take that."

"I'm taking it."

Like everywhere else, the police in Sweden regularly break the law. I was taken to a car and driven to the station with my films in a cage in back. I waited for a long time on a wooden bench before being taken to an office upstairs where a detective investigating the case told me that the police at the airport had informed a prosecutor that my films were terrible and the cops would now view them to determine if I should be

prosecuted for violating some penal code. He said that If convicted, I could be facing two years in prison and a substantial fine for bringing "sick, perverted and terrifying" films into the country.

He asked me some routine questions after telling me I had the right to remain silent. I called the American consulate in the presence of a translator and informed the ambassador I had been subjected to an illegal search and seizure by the police without a search warrant and requested a lawyer. He recommended some law firm in Goteborg so I asked for a public defender and was told I would have to wait another two hours for one to show up. The detective in charge of the case, a common, middle-aged bourgeois beaurocrat with a picture of a red butterfly over his desk, informed me, "We were told your films are very violent and bloody. Is that true?"

Thinking about *Army of Darkness*, the movie I'd seen the night before in a local Swedish multiplex in which someone gets his head blown off every five seconds, it was easy to say, "No."

I was then returned to the holding pen for another four hours where I had to sit on a wooden bench to contemplate two years in prison for making movies the police don't like. A drunk was taken out on a stretcher, a couple of young guys were brought in on various charges and the robot-like Swedish pigs going about their business filled me with nausea and revulsion. I was finally told to go upstairs by the head detective.

"You're a free man," he informed me.

"Weren't my movies dirty enough?" I asked.

"Wait... for translator," he responded.

In the office, my legal aid lawyer introduced himself and the translator told me, while the detective spoke in Swedish, that calls had been made to people high up in the Swedish government and he had been informed that this was not a police matter. My possessions would be returned, but I was forbidden to sell any tapes or exhibit my movies in public. If I did, I risked being arrested and prosecuted for violations of the penal code.

"Don't spread these things around," he said.

I didn't bother to tell him about my show in Stockholm at the end of the month.

He asked me to sign a receipt for the films, books and tapes and asked how I planned to get home.

"Could I get a ride back?" I asked.

Two cops came and drove me home.

When I got home, Kajtek asked me, "Did you kill them?"

"Yes, I did," I replied. "No, I'm just kidding."

"Next time, I will take their pistol and shoot them dead. Then they will not take you."

Later, I moved my films to a safe house and hoped the phone wasn't tapped since I'd be showing the movies in Goteborg at a secret screening for invited guests in four days. I hope the police don't find out so I can avoid going to prison.

Nick Zedd (1985) / Roseanne Melo

CHAPTER TWENTY

I have always felt that it is better to give ulcers than to receive them.

Having terminated another fine year of utter horror, I'm ecstatic at the prospect of more revulsion and dread to be experienced this year. Among the many things that happened to me last year, my father died. Actually, that was a thing that happened to him. He lived a long and full life and then died after recovering from a car crash. On a positive note: he was spared from having to see the hospital bills. I spent some time in the hospital as well. It made me want to die. My father had a saying: "A fool and his money are soon parted." I guess he outsmarted those doctors.

My father also once said, "The only man you can really trust is a dead man." I now trust my father. My father and I weren't really that close. We didn't really share the same view of the universe. He was for doing your duty for the company and your family. Being responsible. Paying the bills. Staying out of trouble. Serving other people. Being quiet. I'm for having as much fun as you can before you go. Loudly.

We wrote each other at least once a week. My father usually had an upset look on his face. He always seemed to be slightly uncomfortable after he retired, and had to spend most of his time with my mother. After my father retired he stayed pretty active for the last five years of his life. He was a lot more active than me. Why the hell he'd want to get up every morning at five a.m. when he didn't have to go to work was beyond me. But there were all those weeds to pull out of the ground. And somebody had to walk the dog. In his later years, my father joined a group of men called the Fossils. They'd do book reports for each other.

Whenever we'd be sitting around the dinner table, my father would try to tell a joke. It would always take him too long. My brother, my mother and I would all be daydreaming about other things and then he'd get to the end of the joke and it wouldn't be funny. My father would then laugh. My brother and I would look at each other, then the absurdity of it would hit us and we'd start laughing over the fact that it wasn't funny. My father just thought it took us longer.

You spend your whole life hoping your parents will come around to your way of thinking—hoping they'll wise up and it never happens. I learned to accept my parents. I learned to never talk about anything important when I was around them. My father's funeral was a blast. He got to wear his best suit. He didn't have to talk to anyone. I got to meet a hundred old people I hadn't seen in thirty years. A strange woman with a beautiful body latched onto me at the funeral. She said it was important that I be open to messages from the dead. She said when her father died, she received a message from him. White flowers kept appearing in unexpected places. How supernatural. I don't think funeral parlors are good pick-up spots.

At the burial the minister read the following words from the Bible, quoting Jesus.

"If a man come to me, and hate not his father and mother and wife, and children, and brethren, and sisters, yea, and his own life also, he cannot be my disciple."

I still don't understand what that's supposed to mean.

It's strange how other people's misfortunes can benefit you.

My father's death following his car crash ended up getting me my first used car. A black cat ran directly under this car when I pulled out from the curb. I wonder if that was an omen. After I hit it, there was blood pouring out of the cat's head and it was limping on the corner of the sidewalk at the light. Some guy on a bike started yelling at me.

"You hit it! You hit the fuckin' cat! Stop! Stop!"

I stopped and got out. A crowd began to form.

"Ohh shit! That's horrible! Who did it?"

"Musta been a hit and run."

No, it wasn't a hit and run, asshole. I'm standing here.

I called an ambulance.

"There's a cat lying here bleeding. It just got hit by a car. Could you send an ambulance over?"

"Oh sure, pal."

I got a shoe box and put the cat in the car and drove her to the animal hospital on 65th Street. I went up to the window in the emergency room and behind the counter was a nurse. I put the box on the counter.

"I just hit this cat with my car and she's bleeding."

The nurse looked at me and said, "What do you want us to do with it?" Very funny. "Maybe you can turn it into a puppet."

How 'bout trying to save its life? It looked like the cat had a broken jaw. I couldn't afford to adopt her and pay sixty dollars a day for her hospital stay so I left her there. I hope she made out better than my father.

This fall I toured England showing my movies. I got a lot of great questions from people before the show:

"What's your new movie about?"

"It's about ten minutes. You'll know what it's about when you see it."

Sometimes I wonder what I should say. I could say it's about life and death. That just about covers everything.

The projectionist at one theater said to me, "You sure got a lot of cocksucking in your movies."

Oh really? Ten minutes of cocksucking out of seventy minutes. There's a lot of other stuff too but I guess you didn't notice that.

Yesterday, my girlfriend informed me that she is writing a book entitled, *My Life with an East Village Loser.* I'm glad it's not about me. Maybe it's about her husband. We've been living in Brooklyn for two years. The rent's cheap out here. That's because you get no service. Is it a job requirement that all supers have to be drunks? When we didn't get any heat or hot water for two days, I called the landlord and informed him we'd be withholding the rent until he turned it back on. We got a message on our answering machine the next day.

"YOU MOTHERFUCKER! GODDAMN YOU, MAKING TROUBLE IN MY BUILDING! YOU MOTHERFUCKER... YOU... YOU HAVE RED HAIR! YOU WILL DIE OF AIDS!!"

That's Dobri. The old bastard who takes most of my money every month. We see him lurking around the building sometimes with a bottle of beer filled with vodka. He reeks of booze. One of the tenants beat him up once. He must have mistaken him for a derelict standing in the lobby. Diego, our super, would sit on a sofa on the sidewalk in front of the building getting drunk looking up women's dresses. He'd shout obscenities at them in Spanish. For some reason, that shithead Dobri fired him.

I suppose I should be glad I have a roof over my head. This year I began to understand where the idea for Heaven and Hell came from. Hell is what happens when you have too much fun. You throw up. Hangovers, venereal disease, cirrhosis of the liver, cavities, cancer—the punishment of nature. Then, the more pain you go through, the more likely it is you'll end up trying to believe in God. What else is left? You can't count on doctors.

Or God.